HISTORY OF Kendal AT OBERLIN

"...an entirely new way of life."

RICHARD E. BAZNIK

The Kendal at Oberlin Residents Association
Oberlin, Ohio

Copyright © 2013 by Richard E. Baznik. All rights reserved.

Published by the Kendal at Oberlin Residents Association, 600 Kendal Drive, Oberlin, OH 44074 (www.kaores.kendal.org).

For information, contact the author at richard.baznik@gmail.com.

ISBN: 978-0-692-02031-9

Printed in the United States of America.

Contents

Preface v

Introduction ix

Chapter I: In the Beginning (1987-91) 1

Chapter II: In and Out of the Ground (1991-93) 23

Chapter III: Up and Running (1993-1998) 41

Chapter IV: Developing the Community (1998-2005) 65

Chapter V: Growing the Community (2006-12) 85

Chapter VI: Our Favorite Things 99

Chapter VII: Forward! 153

Appendices 159

Notes to the Text 185

Index of Topics 187

Index of Names 194

About the Book 211

Two of the many banners displayed in downtown Oberlin during 2013 to commemorate Kendal at Oberlin's 20th anniversary. The banners were designed and produced by art students at Oberlin High School.

Preface

No harm's done to history by making it something someone would want to read.
David McCullough in "The Course of Human Events," his 2003 Jefferson Lecture

When John Elder, then president of the Kendal at Oberlin Residents Association (KORA), first spoke with me in fall 2011 about developing a written history of this community, he knew that I had prior experience writing complex history, and he wanted to get the project moving sooner rather than later. Now, nearly two years later, as the book is about to be published, it is clear that his initiative in launching the project at that time was prudent.

Researching and writing a history such as this one falls into a category that deserves to be called "history that talks back." On a daily basis, the author has spent time with the very people being researched and described – and they knew it. It speaks to the nature of this community that few if any of these residents or staff members took occasion to lobby inappropriately to have their activities or special interests given prominence in the history, and virtually none declined to be interviewed or to provide requested information.

At the same time, it's worth noting that Kendal at Oberlin is only 20 years old, and that it has not yet developed a formal archive function for its records. In the absence of this capacity, it was providential for this author that some key sources of information were made available throughout the project. The first of these was a large box of notes, records, and other materials that John Elder dropped off at my cottage in early 2012, shortly after I accepted the assignment. Included were not only his own copies of minutes and agendas from meetings of the Oberlin Retirement Community planning team when he was a member of the group between 1987 and 1989, but also a much larger store of records accumulated by the late resident Anita Reichard. She was also a member of the early planning committee, and she and her husband were among the community's Founders, moving into their cottage in December 1993. As an aside, she also took my wife and me under her wing even before we moved to Kendal, and I consider her the unofficial patron of this history.

Once the project was under way, Don VanDyke was a prodigious source of information. Don had also been engaged with the early planning committee, and he and his wife moved to Kendal in December 1993 as well. More to the point, Don has been an indispensable element in Kendal's administrative team since before he moved in, providing advice and assistance to the chief executive officer and the board. In the course of this he has also handled a large portion of the documents that describe the community's creation and growth, and with CEO Barbara Thomas's support he provided needed information. Similarly, Maggie Stark, Terry Kovach, and JoDee Palmer in admissions and marketing have been generous in giving me access to their information and to their vault of images from Kendal's history. Toni Merleno and Becky Butler in human resources have been helpful with information about long-time staff employees. Barbara Thomas and her staff have been supportive of this project in every way, even at a time when they have also been dealing with pressures from accreditation visits and master planning activities.

The appendices include lists of people who have contributed to this history in important ways. First are the members of the advisory committee who have worked with me to shape the project and to help resolve issues along the way. I owe them more than they know. Second are the long-time residents and staff who agreed to be interviewed for the history, many of whom also pro-

Former KORA president John Elder (left), who designed the logotype for Kendal at Oberlin's 20th anniversary, and fellow resident Priscilla Steinberg display t-shirts produced to celebrate the milestone.

vided copies of relevant documents and memorabilia. Not listed by name are the more than 80 residents who submitted suggestions for inclusion in the history, including items that can be found in Chapter VI, "Our Favorite Things." Taken together, their ideas help define what this community has been and is. Impossible to list here as well, but still important to note, are the many more residents and staff members who have engaged the author in conversations that all begin something like, "When you're writing the history of Kendal, have you thought about…?"

A community like this is perennially interested in its history, of course, and it has generated previous written accounts of Kendal's early years. Resident Demmie Carrell passed along the draft written in the early 1990s by her late husband, Jep Carrell, and Anita Reichard's files included another early draft by Ed Schwaegerle. The "memory book" compiled by Jane Eddy for Kendal's tenth anniversary in 2003, maintained in the library, provided important information. The author of the next history of Kendal will undoubtedly benefit in similar ways from the memory book Jane is assembling this year for our 20th anniversary. Robert Taylor's collection of historical items from the 15th anniversary program he produced in 2008 was a valuable resource as well.

Even with all this input, the project would not have reached print without the strong support of the KORA Council, the elected representatives of Kendal's residents, who agreed early on to provide substantial financial support for printing and related expenses. John Elder and Don Reeves, former and current KORA presidents, respectively, have been encouraging throughout the process, as have the group's past and current treasurers, Joe Palmieri and Ira Steinberg.

I thank my wife, Donna, for her support, encouragement, and the occasional intervention in my work on the history. She has been the first to review drafts, and has brought her own lively perspective on Kendal to the task.

Finally, although a project like this represents contributions from many people, only some of whom are mentioned above, it will inevitably contain some errors. As its author, I am solely responsible for these.

Thanks to all who have helped, and to all who will read this history. You are my partners in this project.

REB

August 2013

Introduction

It is an act of faith every time one of Kendal's prospective residents sells a beloved house, leaves family and community and old friends, parts with familiar pieces of furniture, and comes to live in small quarters, among strangers, and takes up an entirely new way of life.

Eleanor Stabler Clark, a founder of
Kendal at Longwood[1]

WE LIVE IN A WORLD in which some of the societal characteristics we once took for granted have turned into memories, sometimes happily and at other times sadly. A young person's career opportunities are no longer limited by his or her parents' income or social station, but the increased mobility that allows individuals and families to pursue these opportunities means that older family members will often live far from their children and grandchildren and from the friends whose presence made their earlier years so enjoyable. And the demographic trends of the decades since World War II mean that "the elderly" represent a rapidly growing portion of the nation's total population. It is expected that by 2050 one in every five persons in the United States will be over the age of 65.

When Eleanor Stabler Clark wrote 30 years ago about the "act of faith" involved in choosing to relocate to Kendal—for her that meant moving to Kendal at Longwood, near Philadelphia—she was alluding to the spirit in which decisions like this would be made. Most people of her generation grew up not expecting to have to relocate to "retirement communities," assuming that their extended families would be close at hand to provide supportive environments and needed care. Suddenly, it seemed, those assumptions were no longer valid: the generation that had turned back the Axis powers in World War II would have to adapt to a set of subtle but persistent changes in the way they lived their lives.

The mobility and other lifestyle changes that drove these changes have been incorporated into some of the solutions this generation has developed. Continuing care retirement communities (CCRCs), of which the Kendal system is a notable example, represent one such solution. The underlying design of these communities presumes that residents will arrive while they are still able to live independently, and that they can continue to live in the same community as they progress through the stages of advanced aging. Kendal at Oberlin has some residents who spend large portions of the year traveling or living elsewhere, others who need and receive daily attention from nurses and other health professionals, and many at various stages between those extremes. Another of Kendal's characteristics is the willingness, even eagerness, of residents to jump in to initiate activities or address issues that arise, a quality that is addressed in the allegorical account of an early transportation system in this country offered by the late Tom Piraino, an early trustee and resident of the community:

> In the early American west, stagecoaches carrying passengers often sold first, second, and third class tickets. When the stagecoach suffered problems that interrupted its journey, first class passengers remained in their seats while the problem was being fixed. Second class passengers had to exit the stage but did not have to participate in problem solving activities. Third class passengers had to both exit the stagecoach and contribute to helping correct the problem so the stagecoach could re-

sume its journey with all aboard. Let us hope for, and work for, having everyone in our community be first-rate, third-class ticket holders on the Kendal at Oberlin stagecoach.[2]

This book tells the story of the development of Kendal at Oberlin, beginning with the initial planning group meeting in 1987. You will read about meetings and other events, about financial procedures and construction techniques, and about legal, regulatory, and economic issues. These are all important, of course. But notice as well that, among these noteworthy phenomena, a community was being built—intentionally, carefully, and lovingly. Kendal at Oberlin is people, past, present, and future, committed to building that kind of community.

Members of the Oberlin Retirement Community planning group as they met in March 1988, one year after the original gathering at the home of Karl and Ruth Heiser. Front row, from left: Bill Long, Anita Reichard, Karl Heiser, Dorothy Luciano, and Dave Clark. Back row: Pat Sprigg (The Kendal Corporation), Jep Carrell, Ann Jensen, Jim Stephens, John Elder, Lloyd Lewis (The Kendal Corporation), Ed Schwaegerle, and Bill Koeblitz.

Chapter I

In the Beginning (1987-91)

It was January 1987. The same small group was meeting for lunch at the Oberlin Inn. But this week the conversation brought shocking news. It was reported from George Simpson's retirement party that he and his wife were moving to Columbus, that they could no longer manage their large home and necessary health care. Suddenly we realized that every one of us might soon be facing the same problems.

From an undated summary
by Anita Reichard.[3]

GEORGE SIMPSON, a longtime professor of sociology and anthropology at Oberlin College, and his wife, Eleanor, never lived at Kendal at Oberlin, nor were they part of the planning process that led to its development. Yet they must be regarded as the patron saints of Kendal's emergence in Oberlin. They had arrived in Oberlin in 1947, and Professor Simpson had retired from the faculty in 1971 at the age of 67. The couple continued to live in their large, elegant home near the campus as long as they could, and Simpson remained active in his scholarly field.[4]

The group that met regularly at the Oberlin Inn consisted of community leaders, faculty, and others interested in all that transpired—or could transpire—in the town. Little escaped their notice, to the point that some in town considered them a bit too intrusive. All these years later, however, we can be thankful for their attention to the fact that the Simpsons had no options for a retirement community in the town they loved, where they had lived and which they had served for four decades.

Oberlin Retirement Community Group members Bob Thomas (left) and Karl Heiser at an early meeting of the group.

The Simpsons and their predicament represent early data points in a social trend that has changed families and communities across the nation. The generation of men and women who came of age during the Great Depression of the 1930s, and whose careers were entering their finales during the 1970s, had to contemplate a range of retirement options both more exciting and more terrifying than those their parents and grandparents had encountered. The reasons are not mysterious:

- *Life expectancy*. Before the end of the 19th century, life expectancy for newborns in the United States was well below fifty years. In 1880, about the time when the Simpsons' parents were probably born, life expectancy was less than 40. Because of factors such as improved nutrition and health care and changes in the nature of work, life expectancies zoomed upward throughout the 20th century and are now near 80 for newborns.
- *Population mobility*. A century ago, it was highly likely that aging parents could and would depend to a large extent on their nearby adult children and grandchildren for

assistance and care in their retirement years. Since World War II, however, children have increasingly relocated to other parts of the country for career advancement or for "lifestyle" reasons, and today the notion of the extended family network often depends for its continued existence on some form of advanced technology.

- *The structure of health care.* With the introduction of Medicare and Medicaid in the mid-1960s, health care for the elderly and disabled became increasingly complex, making it almost necessary for many retirees to be engaged with specialists able to navigate intricate policy and procedural hurdles.

As a result of these shifts, persons looking ahead at retirement beginning in the 1980s have faced the prospect of living far longer than their parents did after ending employment, and thus having to rely more and more on retirement savings, pensions, and investments. It is also more likely that they will be geographically distant from their children, and that they will need assistance with the challenges of obtaining continuing heath care and good nutrition and the normal activities of daily life. It is now possible to contemplate an individual's retirement phase lasting as long as or even longer than his or her work career.

Given these developments, it is not surprising that co-housing, a movement that started in Denmark nearly four decades ago, has become attractive to many retirees. The Danish word for co-housing is *bofœllesskabe*, which translates into English as "living community."[5] At its core, co-housing is a way to create a neighborhood of people from a wide variety of backgrounds but with shared values and objectives. Residents live close together, sharing facilities and services. If the community is large enough, it may choose to employ professional management for general administrative duties – but with active participation by residents.

Co-housing communities may be structured as private (either

nonprofit or for-profit) or public entities. Many are operated by or otherwise closely identified with religious groups, while others are nonsectarian or only loosely connected with one or another denomination. In some cases the individual residences are owned privately, while in others the ownership is held in common. Particularly important in this look at the history of Kendal at Oberlin, they accommodate a wide range of options in the interest of giving residents the opportunity to shape their living environment in close collaboration with others.

Early Vision

Many of the societal changes described above were undoubtedly weighing on the mind of psychologist Karl Heiser as he left the lunch group at the Oberlin Inn back in January 1987. A graduate of Oberlin College and a man of considerable intellect, principle, and charm, Heiser was something of a puzzle to many in the community. He had trained as an experimental psychologist, and had traveled widely early in his career, including a trip to the Soviet Union in the 1930s that deeply affected his political attitudes. After holding teaching and administrative positions at several institutions, he and his wife, Ruth, settled in the Cincinnati, Ohio, area, where they opened a clinical psychology practice – a choice forced on them because he refused to sign all the elements of a loyalty oath required of psychological researchers seeking federal grant support during that era.

In 1983, having retired from their practice, the Heisers moved to Oberlin, where they immediately launched themselves into the life of the town and his alma mater. Although the couple was not wealthy in their own right, they found innovative ways to attract funds to Oberlin College. Karl had long been a devotee of Rolls-Royce automobiles, for example, and regularly traveled to England to purchase vintage models to be imported back to the States. It was his practice to drive the car himself for a period, then sell it and donate the proceeds to the College. This allowed him the double benefit of enjoying—with a flourish—the use of a fine car while helping to provide support for his alma mater.

One contemporary observer noted that Heiser's strength wasn't in structure and organization, but rather in energy and vision. The discussion at the Oberlin Inn stirred his interest, and he immediately began a series of conversations with others in the community about how to address the issue of not having retirement community options in town. Before long the beginnings of a solution began to form in his mind, and he decided to pull together a group to work on it. He invited a small number of leading Oberlinians to a meeting at his home on Saint Patrick's Day, March 17, 1987, less than two months after that significant Oberlin Inn discussion had occurred. The letter of invitation suggested a vision that responded to the situation the Simpsons faced: "a home where we can live in comfort and dignity when we become unable to live independently."[6]

Karl Heiser

Attending that meeting, in addition to Heiser, who assumed the role of chair *pro tempore*, and his wife, were the following:

- Jeptha Carrell, executive director, Nordson Foundation.
- Bill Long, former president of the Oberlin City Council and retired director of the Oberlin Coop Bookstore.
- Dorothy Luciano, writer and biomedical scientist (the only surviving attendee of the March 17 meeting).
- Anita Reichard, formerly dean of women at Oberlin College and professor of German at Ashland College.

Also invited but unable to attend the initial meeting were:
- David Clark, vice president for capital development at Oberlin College.
- Diana Roose, assistant dean of the College.
- Elizabeth (Betty) Weinstock, an energetic and resourceful community activist.

The minutes of that first meeting begin with what Heiser surely saw as a clear and compelling call to action: "Agreed that we have a useful idea and should pursue it." Following that entry were fourteen more items outlining assignments accepted by the group's members that would address a wide scope of issues facing the planners: financing, location, information on other similar ventures, primary features of the community, involvement of an architect and a builder, control of the development, health care services and costs, and others. By all accounts, however, Heiser's focus was almost exclusively on the first item.

In the next few months, the planners also took steps to add to their number and to impose some structure on the process. They adopted a name, "The Oberlin Retirement Community" (ORC), elected Jep Carrell as vice chair and Anita Reichard as its secretary and treasurer, and added the following members drawn from the Oberlin community:
- John D. Elder, pastor of First Church in Oberlin.
- James T. Stephens, a retired surgeon.
- Bob Thomas, a retired journalist.

Kendal Connection

From the beginning of the group's work, the concept of a co-housing community of some sort was attractive to the planners, though as they worked through the early review of concepts it became increasingly clear that they were facing a complex set of issues. One of the assignments that Jep Carrell volunteered to take would prove to be particularly significant: he was to call Alan Hunt of Philadelphia, described in the minutes as having "extensive experience in organizing, building, and operating Quaker retirement homes." In fact, Hunt was chair of the board of Kendal at Crosslands, a continuing care retirement community opened in 1977 as a result of discussions begun in the early 1960s in the Philadelphia Yearly Meeting of the Religious Society of Friends. Kendal at Longwood, its older sister community, had opened in 1974. Hunt had also been a college classmate of Carrell and his wife Demmie at Swarthmore College.

Soon after the initial meetings of the planning group, members started to research existing retirement communities, searching for features to be emulated or avoided. In May 1987, Jep Carrell and Jim Stephens traveled to Philadelphia to meet with Alan Hunt and to see the Kendal operation for themselves. They were deeply impressed by what they saw. The Longwood and Crosslands communities seemed to have virtually all the features the planners had been discussing: comfort, dignity, excellent health care, opportunities for interaction with nearby institutions, resident-driven activities programs, and more. They were particularly impressed by Kendal's leadership at the national level, such as the campaign to end the use of restraints for residents in skilled nursing units and an effort to establish a nationwide accrediting program for CCRCs. They returned to Oberlin with glowing recommendations of Kendal as a potential partner.

Based on the outcome of the first visit, a second and larger group of planners—this time adding Anita Reichard, Dorothy Luciano, and Karl Heiser to Stephens and Carrell—organized another trip to Philadelphia in June. They saw and agreed with everything Stephens and Carrell had reported, but encountered something they hadn't anticipated: it didn't look like it would be easy to convince Kendal to play a role in developing a retirement community in Oberlin. Their conversation with Lloyd Lewis, executive director of the Kendal Communities, was informative but not encouraging. In short, Kendal wasn't looking for more sites. They had added Philadelphia-area "sister communities" to the Crosslands, and were already in discussion with a group in Hanover, New Hampshire, the home of Dartmouth College, to develop a Kendal site there. Lewis was not eager to accept an additional assignment, particularly one so geographically remote from Kendal's current locations. The reaction surprised the visitors, but it didn't stop them.

"What would it take to get you to Oberlin," Heiser asked Lewis. The response was both simple and very difficult.

"Get a list of 250 people each willing to put down a refundable deposit of $1,000," Lewis suggested.

Taking Names

With Lewis's response, the Oberlin delegation recognized that their role had changed from planning to recruitment, a focus that would dominate their activities over the coming years. They returned and shared what they had learned with the other members of their group, and together they launched the effort to find at least 250 people willing to invest in their vision for a retirement community. That effort took many forms. At one extreme, Joseph Reichard, Anita's husband and retired professor of German at Oberlin College, wrote to every student on his class grade books from 1948 or earlier. At the other end of the spectrum, plans were made for a large-scale meeting at First Church on June 24, 1987, featuring Alan Hunt of the Kendal Communities, who would describe the Kendal approach to developing and operating retirement communities. Members of the planning group set about identifying any and all local residents and other alumni and friends of Oberlin who might be willing to attend the meeting. Anita Reichard's minutes for the June 10 meeting were simple and direct on this matter:

Picnic with early "priority list" members, one of many events held in northeast Ohio and elsewhere in the country to help future Kendal residents get to know each other before moving into their new homes.

> All were reminded to turn in as many names as possible—even names of some who might not be able to afford that type of living—because their children might make it possible.

That last phrase in Reichard's minutes conveys an important element in the group's thinking: the notion that decisions by aging parents to enter Kendal or another continuing care retirement community would be welcomed by their children, who might be concerned about how to provide support and care in their latter years. Testimonials from family members of residents in subsequent years have validated this assumption many times over.

Attendance at the June 24 meeting at First Church with Alan Hunt was about 150, well beyond what the planners had expected, and the response was overwhelmingly positive. At a follow-up meeting the next morning, Alan Hunt told the committee that they were already ahead of where other groups had been at this stage of their planning – they had more possible sites identified, and some options were opening up for health care that would make their campus increasingly attractive.

The euphoria generated by the gathering at First Church also reigned briefly at the next meeting of the committee on July 1, but the group quickly turned their attention back to the search for 250 people willing to make an up-front commitment to the retirement community. A major element of that search was to be a questionnaire sent from Oberlin College to thousands of its alumni. David Clark, who had been a member of the planning group from the beginning, had been working on drafts of the questionnaire and an accompanying letter, which he was to sign.

Clark's involvement in the project was crucial in several respects. First, he was a senior officer of the College, the town's anchor institution and largest employer, and a major potential drawing card for future residents of the retirement community. Second, he was a fund-raiser, experienced in framing appeals to donors for financial support for worthy causes. And third, his role at the College had grown to include the acquisition of "strategic properties," real estate parcels that the College might acquire through gifts or direct purchases to support future institutional expansion and other priorities.

The questionnaire was not issued until February 1988, however – an early example of the Oberlin group's divergence from some of Kendal's standard methods. Kendal's Lloyd Lewis noted that the methods used to communicate with potential residents for the project in Hanover, New Hampshire, had not included a questionnaire, but rather a letter describing the concept and a response card for expressions of interest. In a July 17, 1987, letter to planning group secretary Anita Reichard, Lewis explained that the Hanover process had yielded an enormous return, and he felt that a similar approach in Oberlin might well be just as successful. The group went ahead with its questionnaire nonetheless. In retrospect, this apparent intransigence, along with other instances of disagreement over approaches to planning issues, may have endeared the Oberlin group to Lewis.

Getting Formal

Since its initial meeting, the planning group had been operating informally, simply as an assembly of people with a shared interest. They had yet to receive or spend any significant resources beyond those they could cover themselves, and they had not been in a position to sign any official agreements or contracts. This was about to change.

By August 1987, the group had enlisted the help of attorney Frank Carlson to prepare an application for incorporation as a nonprofit charitable organization in Ohio. They had also begun discussing potential members of the corporation's board of trustees, people who would bring the skills and experience necessary to launch and lead the enterprise. Karl Heiser had already declared himself not the right person to continue to chair the effort, and had appointed Jep Carrell, John Elder, and Jim Stephens as a committee to develop a slate of candidates for consideration for a board. Meanwhile, in Philadelphia, Alan Hunt was preparing a draft agreement between Kendal Management Services and what was still being called "The Oberlin Group."

Carlson's work on the incorporation process moved along rapidly, and he presented his draft papers at the October 6, 1987, meeting of the planning group. The only part of the draft that drew discussion was the section about "furnishing financial security for persons who become unable to pay the normal charges." After discussion, however, "it was decided that this statement should stand." The issue led eventually to the formation of the Residents Assistance Fund, a crucially important feature of Kendal at Oberlin that is supported by gifts from residents and non-residents alike, and through the sale of items in the RAF Shop and the Cardinal Shop. The final version of the code of regulations added the qual-

The real estate selected as the site for Kendal at Oberlin consisted mostly of farmland just north of the center of town. The northern portion of the land was located in Russia Township and had to be annexed. The approximate boundary of the campus is shown by the dotted line.

ifier "to the limits of its ability to do so" to the Oberlin Retirement Community's commitment to support residents whose resources are no longer sufficient to meet regular charges.

Shortly after the October 6 meeting, Carlson filed papers with the Ohio Secretary of State to form a nonprofit corporation bearing the name "Oberlin Retirement Community." The group resolved that this name would suffice for the time, and that a formal name for the site would be chosen later. The incorporators (Ohio law requires three) were Jep Carrell, Anita Reichard, and Jim Stephens. In the minutes for the October 20, 1987, meeting of the planning committee, Anita Reichard recorded the milestone:

> Although no one has heard officially, it can be assumed that we are now incorporated. Frank Carlson had said that as soon as our papers reached the Secretary of State we could consider the incorporation in effect…

Meanwhile, Alan Hunt had forwarded to the planners a draft agreement between the Oberlin planners and Kendal-Crosslands, the legal name of the entity Kendal had formed to work with developing sites. At that point the model being used in the drafting process assumed that Kendal-Crosslands would own the site, although in the end this was not the case: land and buildings are owned by the nonprofit corporation Kendal at Oberlin. By early November the agreement was finalized, and Lloyd Lewis was able to communicate this news to the hundreds of prospective residents on the mailing list maintained by Kendal Management Services (KMS), the unit created by Kendal-Crosslands to handle various administrative tasks.

During its meeting on December 1, 1987, the ORC board elected its first slate of corporate officers:

>James Stephens, president
>William Koeblitz, vice president
>Anita Reichard, secretary
>Edward Schwaegerle, treasurer

With these actions, the little group that had met at Karl Heiser's invitation almost nine months earlier became the legitimate, credible precursor of the community that exists in Oberlin today. They couldn't have known at that time, however, that those nine months would be multiplied eight times over before the community was designed and constructed and the first residents would move into their new homes.

Recruitment

With its legal structure in place, the board's efforts were focused on the process of identifying 250 or more prospective residents of the new retirement community who would be willing to make the necessary financial deposit. They were aided unexpectedly by a growing awareness of new retirement trends in national media.

Dr. James Stephens, ORC planning group member and first chair of the Community Board for Kendal at Oberlin, shown with Diana McCord, the community's first full-time administrator, at a 1990 picnic for prospective residents.

Opposite: Board members Dorothy Luciano, Anita Reichard, Ed Schwaegerle, and Jim Stephens examining early plans for Kendal.

The November 29, 1987, issue of *The New York Times*, for example, included a major article headlined "Retirees Resettling in College Towns," with a subtitle that proclaimed, "The Life is Full and Housing is Often Priced Reasonably."

The *Times* article and other media coverage called attention to two important trends. First, retirees were returning to the communities where they had attended college, often not to move into retirement communities there but simply to find housing in an environment where they had spent some of the most enjoyable years of their lives. Second, this pattern was evident not only in the Sun Belt states long seen as magnets for retirees, but in Michigan, New York, Vermont, New Hampshire, and Massachusetts. James O. Freedman, then president of Dartmouth College, noted the significance of this development: "This trend speaks well for a change in the sense of values of some Americans considering that it was only recently that retirement to the golf courses of Sarasota and Scottsdale had been considered to be the ideal."

The ORC board members knew that there was interest in a retirement community in Oberlin. Attendance at their information sessions had been strong, and correspondence from prospective residents was positive. Yet the deposits were coming in more slowly than they had expected, reaching $65,000 by November

1987. During a two-day visit in January 1988, however, Kendal's Lewis reported that their progress was good compared to other sites, and encouraged the group to take greater advantage of the communication services available from KMS.

The effort to generate leads was soon ramped up. Dave Clark mailed letters to thousands of Oberlin College alumni from the classes of 1920-1950 in February 1988, and Dorothy Luciano wrote to almost one thousand others in Lorain County. Within a few weeks the group had received responses from more than 1,200 prospective residents, more than half of whom were from outside Lorain County, and more than a third from outside Ohio. While not all of these post cards would ultimately be converted into deposits, the numbers began to allay the concerns of the board.

Location, Location, Location!

Even as the recruitment effort was gaining momentum, the board was engaged in a review of potential sites for the community. Discussion of this topic began shortly after the initial planning

From left, Shirley Hull, Loraine Deisinger of The Kendal Corporation, Jean Wright, administrator Diana McCord, and ORC planning group member John Elder examined an early model for the campus of Kendal at Oberlin.

group agreed the basic concept for the retirement community was sound. Clark provided key leadership for the effort, drawing on his role as the College's lead officer for "capital ventures" as well as his long experience in fund-raising, including seeking and accepting gifts to the College consisting of real estate parcels.

The priorities identified by the ORC board and the Kendal experts focused on selecting a site that would be large enough—probably about 100 acres—to accommodate the scale of development envisioned, would have the necessary features (e.g., sewers and water), and would be as close as possible to the center of town and to the Oberlin College campus, all characteristics that the planners had determined to be crucial. In addition, the matter of cost was important, since the community was just starting and did not yet have any significant capital. This was made more complicated because, as a small town, the real estate market in Oberlin was particularly sensitive to any suggestions that specific parcels of land were under consideration. The planners did not want the price of land to rise simply because they were searching for a site for the community, even as they certainly had to look for sites to be considered.

Because Clark had been involved in discussions with land owners throughout the community on behalf of the College, he was ideally suited to lead the effort on behalf of the planners. The College's continuing interest in gaining control of key real estate for its own purposes was well known in town, and was already factored into asking prices for many parcels. But even Clark found it useful to rely on a local real estate broker to investigate and assemble potential sites for the retirement community. Later there were suggestions that there had been a "disinformation" campaign to mislead town residents about the planners' preferences in location, including a comment attributed to the College's then-president S. Frederick Starr that "Dave Clark and Jim Stephens [the ORC board chair] were out on the sidewalk near Presti's [restaurant on the west side of Oberlin] looking at large rolls of maps." According to Clark, this was not true.

After much sleuthing, the planners had identified three sites that seemed possible. As described in the minutes of the January 5, 1988, meeting of the ORC board, they were:

- A 52-acre site on the west side of Oberlin with good access; a "swap" could provide more access, but a six-acre "buffer" would be quite expensive.
- A 100-acre site on the southwest side of Oberlin with excellent drainage was priced inexpensively, but sewer and water tie-ins would be expensive to build, as would road accessibility.
- A new alternative site of 58+ acres, bounded by Maple, Lorain, and Park Streets and the air traffic control center operated by the Federal Aviation Administration.

As initial planning for the institution that would become Kendal at Oberlin neared an important milestone, Karl Heiser (left), who convened and led the planning group's initial activities, conferred with Thomas Piraino, a lawyer and executive who would later assume the chairmanship of the community board.

Although it was smaller than 100 acres, the third option appeared to offer the most advantages, and it would be possible to acquire additional adjacent land to enlarge the space available for development. But negotiations over the next year failed to yield agreement by the owners of the key parcel in the site, so the planners moved their focus slightly north to another set of parcels offering about 100 acres, much of it outside the city limits of Oberlin. After research to determine what the prospects would be for annexation of the land by the City of Oberlin, the planners gave the signal to Dave Clark to ask the College to begin acquiring the property for the new retirement community.

It wasn't until early 1989 that the needed parcels were at long last acquired. ORC board chair Jim Stephens issued a triumphant message to all those on the priority list announcing that the land had been secured and that more than half of the needed deposits were in hand to allow the land use planning and architectural design to begin. Most of the land had either been woods or farmland, however, and because more of it was classified as "wetlands" than had been expected, this meant that more mitigation and very careful land use planning would be needed. These measures are evident in the placement of buildings, ponds, marshes, and meadows in the completed development.

Early Financing

For about half a year after the St. Patrick's Day meeting in Karl and Ruth Heisers' home in 1987, the members of the planning group had access to no financial resources other than their own. This meant that any activities during that period had to be conducted with an eye toward economy – and ideally at no cost. Most meetings took place at the members' homes or at First Church or other community institutions, and the members themselves supplied meals and refreshments as needed. It was not until the group found it necessary to retain an attorney to begin preparing incorporation papers and to travel to Philadelphia and elsewhere that they decided to assemble a pot of funds to finance the growing scale of activity.

True to form, the group's first step was to look to their own members for needed support. At the September 4, 1987, meeting of the planning group, Dave Clark suggested that the group needed what he called "fertilizer money," funds that could be used to hire needed services, to pay for travel, and perhaps even to secure options on some parcels of land. Using Clark's language, they established a "Fertilizer Fund" consisting of at-risk commitments of $5,000 each from the group's members and from a few other supporters, of which only half was actually drawn down for use. In the end, 15 loan commitments were made by supporters.

Administrator Diana McCord making a presentation to prospective Kendal residents in 1991 at the home of Ed and Ruth Schwaegerle.

When the first round of formal financing was obtained in 1990, the entire amount of these loans that had been drawn down was paid back to the lenders.

The need for larger-scale financing became clear as the project edged closer to reality. In consultation with the staff experts at Kendal Management Services, the planners determined that they needed venture capital—defined as at-risk funding, provided either as a loan or as an investment—of about $2 million to be used for such purposes as obtaining the skilled nursing beds that the community would need and negotiating other arrangements. Because the retirement community was being designed as a nonprofit, the decision was to seek loans rather than investments.

Oberlin College president Starr initially said the College would loan the needed funds at standard venture capital rates (one per cent per month on the committed amount, plus 30% on the amount of the commitment actually drawn down), reflecting the high risk associated with the venture. But the College ultimately decided that the full amount of the financing was too much for its circumstances, and its participation was reduced to $1 million. The town's longtime local medical establishment, Allen Memorial Hospital (now Mercy Allen), reassured by a pledge from an anonymous local donor that constituted a guarantee against loss, agreed to provide the remaining funds on terms similar to those associated with the College's loan.

On a truly remarkable day in March 1992, Joseph and Anita Reichard, both of whom had been key players in the planning efforts that led to the creation of Kendal at Oberlin, joyfully dug into the dirt at the official groundbreaking ceremony. Both of the Reichards were among Kendal's founding residents.

Chapter II

In and Out of the Ground (1991-93)

In January 1991, I couldn't begin to imagine what this so-called Kendal at Oberlin community was all about. The Kendal Corporation staff would come and go, always reassuring me of what a wonderful community this would be.

Marcia Heckert, in July 2003[7]

L‌LOYD LEWIS, CEO of The Kendal Corporation, believed firmly that it was important to develop a sense of community before residents moved into a new Kendal. Thus the marketing efforts of the planning group, in collaboration with the Philadelphia-based corporate staff, were designed to bring prospective residents into contact with each other through meetings and events, newsletters, and other mechanisms. Groups of residents who would be among the first to move in also had opportunities to travel together to Kendal's Crosslands or Longwood communities in Philadelphia to see their layouts and programs, and to a flower show in Columbus, Ohio. In both cases these were activities that helped to nurture the community-building process. By sharing their hopes as well as concerns, they were able to jump-start the kind of relationships that traditionally emerge only after long experience as neighbors or colleagues.

In this approach, Kendal was in the vanguard of a movement dating from the early 1980s through the work of people such as M. Scott Peck, and later in the writing of sociologist Robert Putnam. Neither had focused on retirement communities, but the concepts of community building they advocated were a good fit.

Platform party at the March 16, 1992, groundbreaking for Kendal at Oberlin. From left: Oberlin College vice president David Clark, Kendal Corp. project manager Patricia Sprigg, Kendal at Oberlin administrator Barbara Thomas, Kendal Corporation CEO Lloyd Lewis, Oberlin College president S. Frederick Starr, Oberlin councilman Calvin White, planning group leader Dr. James Stephens, and David Hewitt of The Kendal Corporation.

Between 1988 and 1993, dozens of volunteer workers engaged in the Kendal at Oberlin project were busy recruiting residents. Their efforts were synchronized with activities at The Kendal Corporation's offices in Philadelphia, where descriptive literature was produced and contact information for prospects was placed in data bases. Among the volunteers involved in this process, Anita and Joseph Reichard were key. She was a former dean of women at Oberlin College and professor of German at Ashland College, and he was a retired professor of German at Oberlin. Both had extensive networks among alumni, as well as long experience as leaders of various religious and civic groups. In particular, Anita Reichard's personal notes to prospective residents who attended meetings to discuss plans for Kendal at Oberlin were a mark of her approach. "You have picked an exciting time to join us," she

Above: Kendal at Oberlin board member Anita Reichard sliced the ceremonial cake at a March 16, 1992, groundbreaking party, five years after the initial planning group meeting.

Right: Detailed image of the cake portraying the Heiser Community Center, which functions as the main building of the complex.

wrote to a Michigan couple, "for the project is really beginning to move. There are now some 355 on the priority list, about 200 of whom want to move in 'upon opening....'" Her messages to prospective residents brought Kendal to life for them.

The meetings to which prospective residents were invited took place throughout Ohio, of course, but also in Pennsylvania, New York, Michigan, New Jersey, Illinois, Virginia, Maryland, Washington, DC, Wisconsin, and elsewhere. Attendance varied from a handful to more than 150. At most of these events, one or more members of the Oberlin planning group were on hand to talk about the concept, sometimes accompanied by staff of The Kendal Corporation as well. In every case the names and contact information for interested attendees were cataloged for use with follow-up mailings and other communications to prospects.

Administrative coordination for the emerging Kendal at Oberlin community was handled largely by staff designated by The Kendal Corporation in Philadelphia. Patricia Sprigg, who had been named project director for Kendal at Oberlin in spring 1988 and was later designated as senior administrator, was a constant presence throughout the start-up phase, although Lloyd Lewis was frequently involved as well – both from his base in Philadelphia and from time to time in local meetings in northeast Ohio. By early 1990, Sprigg was the principal Kendal corporate presence before gatherings of prospective residents.

Control over the production and distribution of marketing materials was a regular source of contention between the Oberlin planners and the Kendal corporate staff during this period. To ensure consistency and accuracy, the Philadelphia staff wanted to centralize writing and design of all printed materials, which they would ship off to Oberlin as needed by the local volunteers. From the perspective of the volunteers, however, this arrangement was prone to delays and other problems traditionally associated with "long supply lines." Sprigg soon found herself having to arrange for weekend shipments of materials to arrive in time for the many marketing meetings with prospective residents.

Concrete Steps Forward

Meanwhile, even as these organizational issues were being resolved, there was significant progress during 1991 on a number of issues that were crucial to the new community's development.

As the project moved forward in Oberlin, Kendal acted to hire Diana McCord as the full-time administrator for the new community. She had held a similar position at another retirement community in South Carolina, and her experience was a good fit. A full-time staff leader for the project was an important element at this stage, as the project was selecting architects and finalizing a wide range of other details for the new community.

Dr. Jeanne Stephens, a key figure in the planning for the development of Kendal at Oberlin, lent a hand at the groundbreaking ceremony. She and her husband were founders of the Oberlin Clinic and provided guidance in designing Kendal's health and wellness program.

Marcia Heckert, one of the earliest staff members of Kendal at Oberlin, shown here at her desk in the office the community opened in 1991 on the third floor of a bank building at 5 South Main Street in downtown Oberlin.

The Kendal Corporation's own staff designers provided a set of preliminary concepts for the layout of the new community, giving the local planners a basis for reaching conclusions on matters such as the appropriateness of the site, the nature of the architectural work to be done, and an estimated budget for the project. Based on these preliminary concepts, the planners began working on long-term financing for the new community. The estimated total budget for all development and construction costs was $40 million, a portion of which was expected to be provided by the entrance fees that would be paid by early residents. The balance would be financed by issuing tax-exempt long-term bonds, to be paid off over twenty or more years using revenue received in the out years. To allow development to proceed before collecting entrance fees from all committed residents, The Kendal Corporation arranged for the Oberlin project to be financed temporarily by the Bank of Ireland, a $40 million loan that was repaid within months, as soon as the planners were able to negotiate the issue of tax-exempt bonds through Lorain County.

Based on the preliminary work performed by Kendal's in-house architectural team of Tim Reed and Tom Miller, and using actual expenses already incurred and reasonable forecasts of revenue, the budget for the project in 1991 was estimated as follows:

Expenses:
Project development and construction $40,708,648
Projected debt service reserve 2,494,000
Working capital... 1,124,765
Total expense... $44,327,413

Revenues:
Entrance fees received prior to opening $13,455,000
Entrance fees received at move-in 1,512,378
Interest income... 2,160,035
Tax-exempt bonds (long-term) 15,200,000
Tax-exempt bonds (five-year) 12,000,000
Total revenues $44,327,413

These numbers were daunting to the Oberlin planners, but they were able to draw on the experience of The Kendal Corporation's leaders in developing existing communities. Among the characteristics of Kendal-related retirement communities, for example, was that their residents seemed to live longer than would be projected on the basis of traditional national data. By conducting regular actuarial analyses, Kendal was able to adjust its fee structures as needed to avoid financial disaster, while many other retirement communities that ignored these demographics found themselves on the ropes. This pattern of regular actuarial reviews has continued throughout Kendal at Oberlin's existence, often leading to amusing conversations, as in 2012 when a 102-year-old resident let out a whoop on hearing that the average Kendal at Oberlin resident would probably live for 14 more years.

Actuarial analyses are only one of the measures that Kendal takes to ensure its financial soundness. Others include constant attention to the occupancy rate, controlling operating expenses, and altering fees to reflect inflationary forces. Occupancy rates at Kendal at Oberlin have traditionally run higher than at many other retirement communities, but the admission and marketing staff watches this indicator closely, as well as other market conditions and shifts in health care policy, so it can act when needed to offset cyclical downturns.

Architecture

Architect selection was complicated. The Kendal Corporation's Lloyd Lewis, concerned that the new community be financially successful, wanted the project in Oberlin to adopt design and construction standards that were already working well at Longwood and Crosslands, the prototypical Kendal communities in the Philadelphia region. Reflecting the idiosyncratic nature of Oberlin's traditions, however, the local planners were anxious to work with an architect who would design a distinctive community environment, one that would help achieve social, environmental, and quality of life goals. They felt that they should have a much stronger role in the selection process than Lewis described for them. This tension continued at a low level for many months, punctuated by occasional mentions in communications from Philadelphia or in the minutes of the Oberlin planning group.

After months of arm-wrestling over this issue, the parties agreed on a selection process that started with a review of potential architects by the Kendal staff, which led to the recommendation of the Cleveland-based firm William A. Dorsky Associates. The Kendal at Oberlin Community Board then had a chance to review the firm's proposal and qualifications, and it approved. In the words of Community Board chair Jep Carrell, "the basis for the choice was the firm's experience with design of retirement

Detail from the architect's preliminary elevation drawing for the Heiser Communty Center, the focal point of Kendal at Oberlin.

communities, its acceptance of Kendal's design values and parameters, and its general competence and integrity."[8]

The lead architect for the project was a woman, Cornelia C. Hodgson, a partner in the Dorsky firm (which shortly afterward became known as Dorsky Hodgson Parrish Yue). She was already known widely for her work on senior living environments, and she found herself battling with Kendal's Lewis on how and whether to include features she knew would be highly desirable to the future residents of the new community.

Working with the Kendal staff architects' preliminary concepts and drawing on the experience of Longwood and Crosslands, as well as on the opinions of members of the Oberlin planning group, the architects developed a design for the campus with the following significant elements:

- A land-use plan for the entire area that met all wetlands requirements and also responded to the planners' demands for environmental responsibility, attractiveness, and efficiency.
- 200 independent living units, including 152 cottages built in clusters of four and 48 apartments.
- Five different models of independent living units, from one-room studios to the largest – two bedrooms and a

den. The plan called for these models to be mixed within the cottage and apartment areas.
- A community building with shared facilities for dining, gathering, recreation, library, health clinic, exercise, etc.
- A health care building with both assisted living and nursing care beds, including related dining and activity spaces.
- Indoor swimming pool accessible from all areas.
- Underground utility lines, covered walkways, and some covered parking.
- An attractive external appearance, approved by Oberlin's architectural review process.

Township, City, County, State

From the early phase of the planning process, it was clear to leaders of The Kendal Corporation that Oberlin would be a good site for a new Kendal facility, albeit one that was further west than the organization had expected to venture at that stage in its existence. David Hewitt, a member of the board of The Kendal Corporation and briefly president of the board of Kendal at Oberlin, said in 1991 that the Oberlin location was "an ideal site for a retirement center."[9]

Note that in recent years a second Kendal has been developed in Ohio (in Granville, just east of Columbus), and another further west in Chicago (the Admiral at the Lake).

Although the new retirement community in Oberlin would be a private, nonprofit corporation, it was required to work with several levels of government to address regulatory and financial issues before proceeding:

State of Ohio: In the early 1990s, a federally mandated pattern of regional "health systems agencies" was still in place, requiring hospitals and nursing homes to apply for permission for capital building and expansion projects in order to qualify for governmental reimbursements. Permission took the form of a "certificate of need" (CON). The CON process had been largely abandoned by the time Kendal at Oberlin opened, but the planners needed to go through the steps anyway. A CON was ultimately granted, although in fact Kendal purchased the local Carter Nursing Home and transferred its nursing bed licenses to the new campus, thus technically obviating the need for a CON.

Lorain County: As noted earlier, Kendal's long-term financing plan depended on the county's approval to issue tax-exempt bonds. The county also had to approve the annexation of the Kendal site into the City of Oberlin, as well as the tax-exempt status of the new campus.

City of Oberlin: Here the issues were even more complex, beginning with the annexation of land for a portion of the new campus from the adjoining Russia Township and the question of how much of the new campus would be exempt from taxation. These were significant issues, but they paled in comparison to the concern over the lack of adequate water and sewer capacity to serve the new campus. Overcoming this obstacle meant that the city would have to build about 1,000 feet of new utility lines to the site, a major capital expense. Extended negotiations finally worked out a way to pay for the project through utility payments over time. Finally, much of the campus area would need to be rezoned from "residential" to "planned development," a change that had consequences for the city's long-range land use plans.

New Russia Township: Oberlin is surrounded by townships, all much smaller in population and largely rural in nature. Before 1992, Russia Township was part of the city of Oberlin, but in that year its residents voted to separate from the city and adopt the name "New Russia Township."[10] To assemble its campus, Kendal proposed the annexation into the City of Oberlin of 42 acres of

Above: Kendal at Oberlin Executive Director Barbara Thomas (left) discussed construction progress on site with Kendal Corporation CEO Lloyd Lewis and construction manager Tom Mitchell in September 1992.

Below: By April 1993 construction had moved forward significantly, as seen in this view of the campus looking toward the southwest from the driveway to the Heiser Center. The photo also illustrates why Kendal long-timers often refer to the period prior to construction as "before dirt" or, referring to heavy spring rains, "before mud."

land then located in New Russia Township. Township trustees listened to plans for the new retirement community and agreed to the annexation request.

Particularly at the state level, Lloyd Lewis, Pat Sprigg, and other Kendal executives provided assistance to the Oberlin planners in dealing with governmental issues. But even at the state level, the planners were directly engaged in negotiations. This was especially true in the matter of the CON process, where a subcommittee led by Dorothy Luciano, together with John Elder and Karl Heiser, devoted much time to learning the ins and outs of regional health planning approval processes.

In the Ground…

Groundbreaking for the new campus took place on March 16, 1992, somewhat later than the planners had hoped but necessary to accommodate all the negotiations described above. The late Connie Flanigan Boase, an Oberlin resident and one of Kendal's "Founders," reported that she and other local residents had been a bit uncertain about whether Kendal would actually come into being, but the groundbreaking eliminated all doubts. The actual campus area was used for the ceremony, but participants went immediately afterward to the warmer and more comfortable surroundings of First Church on Oberlin's Tappan Square for a reception to celebrate the start of construction.

Anxious to make up time lost in the approval and negotiation processes, the construction phase moved along rapidly, slowed only by a rough winter in 1992-93. The construction site was filled with mud much of the time, but eager prospective residents arrived frequently to look around. During this period the headquarters staff for the new Kendal community occupied office space in a bank building in downtown Oberlin, and interested prospects were encouraged to come by that location for information, but they continued to visit the new site of the campus as well.

The first residential component of the campus to be built was a set of eight cottages, numbered #1 through #8, located closest to the main entrance to the entire site. In the downtown office the staff had been able to show prospects models of the living areas and drawings of all spaces, but access to the "real thing" was far better. As soon as possible the office was relocated to cottage #1 and began operating from there.

Marcia Heckert, who had joined the fledgling Kendal at Oberlin staff in January 1991 as an assistant and who remained at Kendal for nearly two decades, later recalled the planning and construction period as a time of rapidly shifting forces and continuously moving groups of staff and volunteers. In early 1992 her supervisor, administrator Diana McCord, left the position, and Philadelphia-based project manager Pat Sprigg filled in until a replacement administrator could be recruited.

The person hired in March 1992—just two weeks before the groundbreaking—as the community's new administrator was Barbara Thomas, who brought with her considerable experience as a senior manager at the Judson Retirement Community in Cleveland. She hadn't been seeking another position. Rather, she was approached by Kendal after she led an accreditation team visit to Kendal at Longwood and Crosslands, where she met Lloyd Lewis. On that visit she saw a self-study for a potential Oberlin site and knew at once that it would be competition for Judson. When Lewis later approached her about the Oberlin opening and provided information about Kendal's approach, she was immediately impressed with its values, resident-driven culture, and sense of history. She was particularly taken with its restraint-free policy and its emphasis on premier services.

Thomas recalls being interviewed for the job "in a bank building in Oberlin," and that her early months on the job were hectic. First came orientation sessions at The Kendal Corporation in Philadelphia: operations, development, human resources, and more.

Early members of the Kendal at Oberlin staff gathered at the construction site in spring 1993 to view progress. From left to right: Terry Fries, Duane Hamilton, Debbie Kroupa, Barbara Thomas, Therese Hoffman, Trina Schultz, Marcia Heckert, Diann Edwards, and Anne Piccinini.

She understood that 70 per cent of her time from her start day until Kendal's opening would be devoted to marketing to ensure an adequate occupancy rate. She rallied a small group of staff and volunteers around her, including Marcia Heckert, Don VanDyke, a local physician who had worked with the early planning group, Trina Schultz in marketing, and Anne Cunningham as an administrative assistant. She also hired Nancy Freed, a former colleague at Judson, to create press releases and ads.

Shortly after Thomas arrived, Pat Sprigg announced that she was leaving Kendal for a position elsewhere. This was a challenge to Thomas, since Sprigg had been her "main person" in her new position at Oberlin. Thomas has handled periodic changes quite well: as this history is written, she has celebrated her 20th anniversary at Kendal, and when Kendal celebrates its 20th anniversary in October 2013, she will be in her 22nd year as administrator.

...And Out of the Ground

On April 21, 1993, Kendal celebrated an important milestone in the construction of the new campus— the "topping off" ceremony, a custom that indicates that basic construction had been completed for the tallest element of the project, in this case the Heiser Community Center.

Construction workers "top off" the tower of the Heiser Community Center on April 23, 1993.

The program included a morning discussion at First Church and lunch at the Oberlin Inn, followed by a bus caravan to the Kendal construction site. While on the site, guests were instructed to "stay within the roped-off areas," as most of the grounds were too muddy and otherwise cluttered with building materials and equipment to accommodate informal walking tours.

As the summer of 1993 started to turn into early fall, the construction crews that had been working on Kendal's new campus for the past 18 months began to thin out. The rooflines and footprints of the cottages and other buildings were finally evident, although they continued to be surrounded by mud or dust, depending on the weather of the day.

Visits to the new campus by both prospective and committed residents became increasingly frequent, with hardly a day going by without a visiting delegation. Lawns and shrubs were still weeks away, but visitors seemed excited even in their absence – at least they could now see where they would ultimately be placed. The campus design had preserved some of the old-growth trees that were already on the land, but the many new young saplings that would grace the grounds were also months or even years away from arriving.

Earlier in the summer, Barbara Thomas and her colleagues had organized a job fair to recruit staff for Kendal. For many residents of Oberlin, this was the first concrete evidence that the new retirement community would bring benefits to people who were not going to be living at Kendal. Thomas and her colleagues were looking for staff in a wide range of positions: health care, housekeeping, maintenance and grounds, administrative support, food services, and many more. They weren't hiring only Oberlin residents, but they did select many local residents to fill the new positions. Others, like Ann Pilisy, who was hired in early September 1993 to be director of the main dining room (then the only dining room), lived elsewhere but moved to Oberlin several years later. She had previously been the food and beverage director at the Cleveland Athletic Club.

In addition to complying with the architectural design criteria mentioned earlier, the campus of Kendal at Oberlin meets fundamental design principles of the co-housing movement as outlined decades ago by Charles Durrett and Kathryn McCamant, the architects who introduced the concept to the U.S. Among these principles are several that promote a walking environment, including walkways that encourage resident interaction, maximizing common areas, and physical design that encourages intergenerational contact, minimizes the need for cars, and locates parking for cars away from residences.

Mary Lou Thomson adding her signature to the document celebrating the opening of Kendal at Oberlin on October 6, 1993. The document continues to be displayed in the Heiser Community Center.

Chapter III

Up and Running (1993-1998)

The committee will host a meeting of all pet owners early in December. A major problem to be solved is that of "pickup."

Report from the Pet Concerns
Committee in the *Ad Hoc Newsletter*,
November 11, 1993

One of the first committees we heard about was the one that emerged spontaneously when Kendal first opened and there were places to hang coats – but no coat hangers. A "Coat Hanger Committee" announced a need for hangers, and a sufficient number of coat hangers were on hand within a matter of days.

From resident Katie Brown

CONSTRUCTION, FURNISHING, and staff hiring and training continued through the spring and summer of 1993, and the new Kendal at Oberlin campus was finally ready for occupancy in fall of that year. Planning and construction had been long and often stressful, but the end was near.

Ready for Prime Time

"Ready," as it turned out, was a judgment that assumed a hardy, pioneering spirit on the part of the first residents and staff members. The challenges began even before the first new residents were due to arrive on October 4, 1993. It is not unusual to hear founding staff members such as Michele Tarsitano-Amato, direc-

Above: Dave Clark offered remarks before the formal ribbon-cutting for Kendal at Oberlin two days after the first residents moved in.

Opposite: The ribbon was cut by (from left) Barbara Thomas, Oberlin council member Linda Lewis, Ben Custer, Anita Reichard, Oberlin College president S. Frederick Starr, and John Diffey of The Kendal Corporation.

tor of creative arts therapy, say they've "been here since mud" in talking about their tenure at Kendal. This was literally true: when she arrived in August 1993, two months before the scheduled arrival of residents, the campus lacked grass, shrubs, and most of the paving that was planned. Summer rains had produced heavy mud throughout the clay soil campus, but that wouldn't remain the only problem.

"There was not a blade of grass anywhere," wrote resident Samuel Moore, who arrived in early October with his wife Jane. "The wind constantly blew and there was fine clay dust everywhere." Within a few weeks the situation was reversed as rain once again pelted the area: "When we were taking a rest on the patio [after unpacking some items], I stepped off the concrete and got so much mud onto my sneakers that it took my husband an hour and a half to clean it off," wrote Gladys MacKay, who moved

in with her husband during November 1993. "When we have been through so much getting this place started," she continued, "we have wonderful relationships."

Much was yet to be done. One priority was hiring staff colleagues, which was done by conducting interviews in cottages 8-10 because the walls in the care center weren't installed yet. Further, the cottages had not yet been numbered, so Tarsitano-Amato was dispatched to handle that task because the U.S. Postal Service demanded that it be done before any residents arrived. "It was a nightmare," she says, declining to defend a numbering pattern that after two decades seems unusual at best. "Do you number on the basis of someone walking to the cottages from the perimeter road, or from Heiser, or from the proximate parking lot?" The result is a numbering system that puzzles some. In hindsight, Tarsitano-Amato thinks it would have been better to

As part of the ribbon-cutting festivities, resident Esther Hunt (far right) showed off her new cottage to visitors. At the age of 102 as this history is written, she continues to live independently in the same cottage.

let the Postal Service do the numbering so all complaints could be directed toward them.

On another front, the care center rooms had to be certified by Medicare before the first residents moved in. Regulations called for each of the rooms in the care center to include a bed, a lamp, a chair with arms, and other key furnishings. But the inspector interpreted the regulations to mean that every room where a Medicare-financed patient could ever be assigned had to be fully furnished immediately, not only those rooms that were expected to be occupied in the near future. As the inspector toured the various care center wings, staff members carefully moved furniture from the areas that had already been inspected to the rooms yet to be seen. The inspection was completed successfully.

The actual arrival of the first residents, beginning on October 4, 1993, required a carefully choreographed sequence of activities. The idea was that no more than two moving trucks would arrive per day, and that they would be heading to different areas of the campus, the objective being to avoid the congestion, or clouds of dust, or muddy quagmires that would result if larger numbers of trucks, cars, and residents descended simultaneously on a single section of the overall campus. There were some unexpected opportunities for learning, as when two new residents arrived to spend time in the nursing area of the care center, both with broken legs, one left leg and one right leg. The staff found they needed to house them in rooms on opposite sides of the corridor because of the configuration of the showers: each needed to shower with her injured leg hanging out of the shower area, and the spaces were mirror images of each other.

The arrival of Kendal's first residents was celebrated with a ribbon-cutting ceremony on October 6, 1993. Among the speakers at this happy and much-anticipated event was Benjamin Custer. He and his wife, Emiko, had been the first residents to move into their cottages on the new campus on Monday, October 4. Speaking on behalf of all of the community's new residents, Custer described Kendal and the city of Oberlin as places "…where discussion and debate prevail over violence, where music is more available than in the big cities, where library resources are equally so, and where there is a museum not too far behind what the cities offer. Add tender loving lifetime health care, association with stimulating and intellectual friends and neighbors, Quaker ethics, and what more can one ask?"[11]

All those attending the ribbon-cutting event were invited to witness this "commencement" by signing a hand-lettered proclamation, which has been preserved and continues to be displayed in the Heiser Community Center.

Because of their pattern for moving in, early residents often saw very little of each other except at common meals, and meeting neighbors could be a bit random. Nonetheless, the process was effective, as resident Esther Hunt recalled a decade later:

> "My most lasting memories are the deep feelings of relief and satisfaction. At last I was in! My furniture all fit where I wanted it. The stove, the washer, the refrigerator all worked – I knew, because I tried them all. Even more importantly I had already met and talked with a neighbor. I had liked her on sight. I liked her little dog Annie as well. I think all my memories can be described by the one word – Peace."[12]

Since 1993 the Founders have come together regularly to share memories and to update each other on their activities. This has been a valuable element in maintaining the Kendal community.

"How Cold Was It?"

In October, November, and December 1993, following the schedule they had received from Kendal's staff, new residents and their belongings continued to arrive five days a week through December 1993. A total of 187 residents moved into their new homes during that three-month period, a group whose members—many now deceased—are honored to this day with the designation "Founders." (A list of Founders is contained in the appendices.)

As is customary, of course, fall turned into winter, and those early residents soon found themselves dealing as well with one of the most severe winters in northeastern Ohio's recorded history. In January 1994, the temperature dipped as low as -23F, equaling the coldest readings recorded in the city of Oberlin since 1900. A decade later, resident Dorothy Holbrook wrote:

> "The extremely harsh winter of 1993-94 was a trial for people and buildings. One weakness in the buildings was that pipes froze and sprang leaks in the one-bedroom cottages… One afternoon I returned from a meeting just in time to be greeted by

Members of the housekeeping and facilities staffs performed a skit during the first anniversary celebration in October 1994 in which they humorously described the near-heroic efforts they and others had made during the previous winter to clear sidewalks and driveways of snow, and to repair frozen pipes and otherwise keep the community operating through a difficult season. The humor was appreciated, their work even more so.

a stream of water spreading across the carpet. Facility Services to the rescue in a few minutes! (Such a contrast to having to wait days for repairmen for my house!)"[13]

In fact the pipes and aspects of the heating system failed during the deep freeze of that notable winter. Since the construction was new and still under warranty, repairs were made—including modifications in design in some cases—without financial expense to Kendal. But the stress on staff and residents was considerable, even as it provided a shared experience that ultimately promoted a closer sense of community. It also showed residents a dimension of the staff that was both comforting and surprising: faced with such weather extremes, staff from all areas and all levels pitched in to help with chores such as snow removal. Stories are still told of CEO Barbara Thomas shoveling snow at the peak of the cold weather. The February 1994 issue of the monthly resi-

Above: Residents shown with the "Founders Quilt" that they and others made to commemorate Kendal's initial months of operation. From left were Frieda Gabalac, Victoria Young, Nelle Meints, Sadie Taylor, Demmie Carrell, and Ina Jean Kornblith.

Right: Quilt square portraying the result of confrontations between a traffic sign and moving trucks (see text).

dent newsletter, *The Kendalight*, took note of the season's vicissitudes: "Once again we've run out of space without thanking Barbara Thomas and the Thaw Team for the prompt attention to our winter problems."

Some 55 members of the "Founders" group were recruited to design and fabricate a quilt to commemorate the opening of Kendal. The resulting quilt, a large, striking piece of art, hangs in the corridor that connects the Stephens Care Center with the Heiser Community Center, and is often suggested to new residents as a landmark for navigating the halls. Humor played a role among the

Residents Betty Verlie (left) and Norma Daffin staffed a booth with information about the volunteer committee organized in Kendal's early months. The group worked to match residents with the needs of area organizations seeking help from volunteers.

quilters: One of the images on the quilt shows a damaged speed limit sign, recalling the traffic sign that was crashed into not by one but two moving vans during the initial move-in period, after which the sign was moved out of the way.

Early Style-Setting

The concept of resident-initiated activities was built into the model for Kendal at Oberlin by its early planners, and perhaps no other trait so clearly identifies its special character. "No activities director!" was an important plank of the planning group's platform, an attitude that also assumes that residents will get to know each other's preferences and needs and will provide assistance and encouragement as appropriate.

Within a month or so of the arrival of Kendal's first residents, they began a tradition that remains closely associated with the

Above: The first meeting of the Organizing Council, which became the Kendal at Oberlin Residents Association (KORA). From left are Sadie Taylor, Milt Yinger, Joe Verlie, Alan Gage, Art Steele, Lyn Metzger, Frampie Ailey, and Etta Ruth Weigl. KORA is the principal organization representing residents in activities at Kendal.

Below: An early meeting of the recycling committee, including (from left) Lois Peterson, Molly Anderson, staff members Barbara Thomas and Duane Hamilton, Barbara Leonard, and Polly Warch. From its beginning, Kendal at Oberlin residents have maintained an active interest in environmental issues and have advised the community on how best to conserve energy and to protect their surroundings.

community: they began forming resident-led committees to launch and oversee activities of every conceivable nature. While the number of these committees was understandably small in the early years, by the end of five years of occupancy it had grown to 70 or so, and as this history is written the list of committees has grown to almost 90. Some are clearly "ad hoc" or temporary in status, such as the "coat hanger committee" mentioned above, while others are more permanent, often established as formal committees of the residents' association.

A few topics are deemed important enough to have more than one committee. the matter of health eating, for example, is the subject of the Food Committee and the Nutrition Committee, both established by the Kendal at Oberlin Residents Association (KORA), as well as SPINACH, an interest group whose name is an acronym for "Senior People Interested in Nutrition and Community Health." Rather than resulting in overkill, this approach often yields a relatively light touch in confronting issues, such as this August 1997 report from the KORA Food Committee in response to complaints about the "French onion soup" being served in the dining rooms:

> "Problem: French onion soup should have a slice of bread with melted cheese on top.
>
> "Answer: this is not genuine French onion soup.
>
> "Solution: remove the word 'French' from the menu description…"

Another example of multiple committees being formed to address related needs was provided during that severely cold winter of 1993-94. As reported in the December 9, 1993, issue of the *Ad Hoc Newsletter*, residents launched a new set of committees then known collectively as "Care and Concern" (now "Care and Nurturing") to deal with "the personal well-being of Kendal residents." The committees were described as follows:

Residents Jeanne Stephens (left), Shirley Hayward, and Sandra Podwalny staffed a table for the House Committee at an early activities fair for Kendal residents. The committee is responsible for coordinating the selection and placement of furniture and other decor in Kendal's public spaces.

Below: Alan Gage at the front door of his cottage looking over the snow drifts that resulted from a fierce storm in March 1996.

- "The Buddy System: A plan for frequent periodic contact with residents who might develop but be unable to report acute personal problems …

- "A Hazard Reporting Committee, chaired by Lois and Hugh McCorkle…, will be interested in receiving information about actual or potential problem areas in the facility (such as puddles that might freeze, inadequately lighted areas, etc.) They will bring the matter to the appropriate Kendal departments…

- "A Helping Hands Committee… is available to provide companionship and support, if needed, during transportation and waiting time when a resident must be sent off-site for medical purposes…

- "Has frustration, malaise, or loneliness set in? If so, members of the Neighbor-to-Neighbor Committee are ready, willing, and available to lend a helping hand."

Looking back over two decades of operation – and an additional six years of planning – these features of life at Kendal represent legacies from the organizers of the community. The challenges of founding a living environment that would carry its founders' values and its intended culture decades or even centuries into the future are enormous, not unlike those associated with founding a new country. Newly arrived residents may occasionally find it strange that their neighbors spend so much time and energy discussing the traditions and practices that characterize Kendal, but they soon realize that this is simply a way of reinforcing and sharing their commitment.

Getting Together

Inevitably the first several months after Kendal opened saw many activities designed to help new neighbors get to know each other. An example was the "Twilight Holiday Walk" held on the evening of December 11, 1993, during which residents were invited to tour a number of cottages and apartments that were specially opened for the occasion. "There is such a variety, within identical space," the planners of the event noted, "that it should be fun to see them – not to mention the bonus of meeting some new neighbors."

On a larger scale, the first months after the community opened saw efforts to form a residents association, an outgrowth of the formation of the various committees referred to earlier. With a resident population approaching 200, many of them energetically engaged in the effort to build a community, the task of selecting representatives and developing initial policies and procedures for such an association was necessarily complicated. Tom Piraino, chair of the Community Board, as Kendal's governing body was known at the time, wrote to all residents in February 1994 asking them to nominate members of an "organizing council" to take first steps. One month later a slate of eleven, drawn from a pool of 60 nominees, was elected at an "evening exchange" meeting with Barbara Thomas.

At its first meeting, on May 12, 1994, the members of the Organizing Council elected Joseph Verlie as chair, Alan Gage as treasurer, and Dorothy Holbrook as assistant treasurer. They agreed that every resident would be a member of the residents association, and that decisions would be made by consensus, with votes as necessary. The initial statement of purpose for the association was practical and clear: "Because of the overlapping purposes of several Kendal organizations, now in process of change, a strong residents association at KAO is needed."

Over the coming months, the Organizing Council served two roles: developing the basic governing documents for the yet-to-be-created residents association, and functioning on an interim basis as a representative body. In June 1994 the group published a "preliminary summary" of bylaws for an association in *The Kendalight*, and a few months later residents received drafts of a full

Residents Dick Taylor (left), Dorothy Luciano, Ogden Hannaford, and Sadie Taylor examined plans for a swimming pool at Kendal. Hannaford, a retired professor of architecture at Illinois Institute of Technology, developed an aproach to installing a full-sized pool for the community.

constitution and bylaws for consideration and a vote. By the end of September, the first fund-raising letter was distributed to raise funds from residents to support the work of an association. A very large majority of residents contributed to the fund, which ultimately reached a total of $10,552.

In the Water

From its inception, there had been plans to include a swimming pool in Kendal's facilities. There was sharp disagreement, however, on the nature of the pool to be built. The Kendal Corporation's Lloyd Lewis, concerned with construction and operating costs, argued that the pool should be a small, shallow, casual installation similar to those found at many hotels and apartment buildings and other retirement communities. Vocal residents, many

Kendal at Oberlin board chair George Bent applauded as executive director Barbara Thomas presented a shovel to resident Connie Boase so she could turn the first shovel of dirt for the swimming pool groundbreaking.

of whom were serious swimmers and water-walkers, disagreed: they favored a larger, deeper pool, suitable for lap swimming and deep-water exercise.

Lacking consensus, the pool was not among the facilities initially provided for residents who arrived in 1993. Debate continued, however, and it was determined that coming up with a plan to finance the project was the key step. A pool committee, among whose leaders were residents Connie Boase and Etta Ruth Weigl, was formed to serve as a voice for residents seeking an appropriate facility and to assemble an effort to raise funds for the project. Another resident, the late R. Ogden Hannaford, a retired architect, produced a preliminary design for a large pool that placed it in the southwest quadrant of the Kendal campus, adjacent to the Stephens Care Center.

Financing remained a challenge. Then, in September 1994, almost a year after the first residents arrived, the late resident Bill Johnson donated $150,000 toward the construction of a swimming pool. Described in *The Kendalight* as "salubrious" (meaning "contributing to health"), the gift was made in memory of Johnson's late wife, the sculptor Mayo Crew Johnson. Motivated by Johnson's gift and urged on by the pool committee, Kendal's Community Board—the body that later became its Board of Directors—reached a decision later that fall to move ahead with the project:

Resident Etta Ruth Weigl at the July 11, 1996, opening of the new swimming pool, with borrowed vintage swimming suit, bonnet, and parasol.

> We have agreed to settle on… an indoor facility that would include a general purpose/lap pool which is four lanes wide, has appropriate depths and a length of sixty feet; a therapy pool that meets all modern requirements; an exercise room suitable for wellness activities; a hot tub suitable for recreational use; suitable and adequate locker room facilities.[14]

The estimated cost of building the pool was $950,000, to be offset as much as possible by gifts solicited for that purpose, with any remaining balance to be borrowed. In March 1995, KORA's officers wrote to all residents and "Kendal Friends" to encourage additional gifts toward the project budget. Two months later, in

Swimming pool, completed in 1996, almost three years after Kendal at Oberlin opened. The main pool, shown in the foreground, accommodates lap swimming, water walking, and water aerobics classes for residents and community guests. To the right of the main pool is a smaller therapy pool, where the water temperature is maintained at a higher level to soothe aching muscles. The pool is open seven days a week, though users are prohibited from swimming without other people the room.

May 1995, CEO Barbara Thomas wrote to all those who had contributed to the pool and fitness center project to report that the Kendal board had decided to begin construction. The final project budget included $460,000 in gifts and pledges, $400,000 in funding from Kendal at Oberlin, and $228,000 in loans from ten residents. All elements of the project were to be built except for the hot tub: the design would include space and plumbing in case the whirlpool would be added later.

On July 11, 1996, about a year after construction began on the fitness center project, there was a dedication program under the motto "Catch the Wave." The program included a description of the project, offered by Connie Boase, and a "Surf & Turf" demonstration of water walking and lap swimming featuring Boase and Etta Ruth Weigl, the latter sporting a vintage bathing suit. Kendalites finally had their own pool.

The pool was not the only issue around which the residents' opinions differed from those of The Kendal Corporation. Early plans had called for laundry facilities for cottages to be centralized in shared utility rooms, while residents insisted they be located in the individual cottages. On a matter of style, corporate representatives suggested that residents be expected to "dress for dinner" in the main dining room. These, too, were discussions in which the residents' desire to resist standardization prevailed.

"How Are We Doing?"

A key tenet in modern organizational leadership involves regular efforts to check on the perception of the group's services by its constituents—its "customers," some would say. This practice has entered the realm of nonprofit management as well, and it is practiced enthusiastically throughout the Kendal system.

In early 1998, as Kendal at Oberlin was mid-way through its fifth year of operation, the community benefited from a "post-occupancy evaluation" by a team led by Cornelia Hodgson, the architect who had developed and executed the design for the campus. An expert in designing environments for older adults, she had by this time gained a national reputation based in part on her earlier work at Kendal at Oberlin. The report[15] issued by the evaluation team is a remarkable document, assessing the life of the campus as much as the state of the facilities, and including shortfalls and problems along with its many examples of successful design. The picture of residents of the continuing care retirement community that emerges is inspiring:

> "In general, they tend to be younger than most CCRC residents. Research has indicated that the average age for comparable CCRC residents will often range in the low eighties. Oberlin residents have a mean of seventy-five years.
>
> "Not all of Oberlin residents come from Ohio. In fact, residents have moved to Oberlin from a total of twenty-three states. As a result residents are well traveled and have exposure to living in different areas.
>
> "Residents as a group tend to be highly educated as is evident by the alumni or professional status from Oberlin College. Over half of the residents have a connection to Oberlin College…
>
> "A last point of interest is the friendships which a number of the residents have continued with each other. Some of these friendships have lasted sixty years or more…."

In addition to collecting this information about residents' backgrounds, the report also discussed their tendencies to form committees to start or conduct activities, to volunteer both on the Kendal campus and in the larger community, and to stay engaged with issues and changing technology. The authors noted one un-

Residents Ken Roose (left) and Bill Renfrow at the clay-surfaced tennis courts that they and other residents worked to develop after Kendal opened. The clay surface was chosen because it is easier on aging joints.

Resident Doris Sable (foreground) carried an American flag to lead the first Independence Day parade at Kendal on July 4, 1994. Residents and staff decorated wheelchairs, walkers, and themselves to celebrate.

expected phenomenon that continues to confound observers: "One might expect residents to become less active after moving to Kendal due to aging. However, it was found that the longer a person lived at Kendal, the more active in events they became."

Residents' attitudes about their apartments and cottages were largely positive, particularly regarding their overall design, location, and views. After five years of operation, however, there were a number of suggestions for improvement. Most frequently mentioned were a desire for additional parking spaces, including covered parking; different choices for floor covering in the entry areas of cottages; and improved choices generally for materials and architectural detailing. Large numbers of both cottage and apartment residents reported having made changes in their units, most frequently by adding shelving, sun rooms, and lighting.

Attitudes toward the public areas in the Heiser Center were also largely positive, but with some suggestions. The most frequently requested improvement was more small meeting rooms for formal or informal gatherings. Most of the spaces in Heiser were considered too large for the kind of groups that regularly gather at Kendal, and there were too few of them to accommodate demand. Other comments pertained to the design of the auditorium, the acoustics in the dining rooms, natural and artificial lighting, and "way-finding" information (maps and signs).

The items recorded in the 1998 analysis provided a starting point for subsequent improvements in existing facilities, and for the design of new spaces in the coming years. The community was still in its youth, but it now had enough experience to enumerate how it could be even better in the future. In the February 1998 issue of *The Kendalight*, a column entitled "Musings about two events" reflected on comments made at a gathering the previous month to honor Jim Stephens, one of the original planning group members for Kendal at Oberlin. "We could only marvel at how a plan for a small apartment on Hollywood Street [an early alternative plan considered by the planning committee] could turn into our 92 acres of today," the column reported. "Countless meetings alternated between discouragement and triumph, as prospective occupants were lined up, one by one."

The fifth anniversary celebration event, held in Heiser Auditorium on October 8, 1998, featured readings and music performed by residents and staff. The first item on the program was Ruth Shaeffer reading her composition "Owed to Kendal," described as "original verses on the occasion." Contained in that lengthy poem was the following stanza:

> *This is the heart of Kendal, you know.*
> *Our respect for each other, the caring we show.*
> *Such Quaker values we can all share.*
> *They bind us together, making Kendal so rare.*

It's been said that in the first few years of life a child learns a large percentage of everything he or she will ever learn. So it was with a new community of seniors in the town of Oberlin, Ohio.

This view, from 1997, shows an example of the landscaping and gardening that have beautified the Kendal campus since those muddy construction days of 1992 and 1993. Cottage residents who wish to do so are encouraged to cultivate the areas around their units. Facility services staff members handle lawn mowing and care of trees and bushes further away from cottages.

Chapter IV

Developing the Community (1998-2005)

With the distant future in mind the board is taking preliminary looks at the possibility of expansion, both physically here on site and functionally in services to the wider community…
Dorothy Luciano reporting for the Kendal at Oberlin Board of Trustees at the March 1998 meeting of KORA

IN THE FALL OF 1998, as Kendalites were celebrating the fifth anniversary of the grand opening, the community had begun to settle into a comfortable yet exciting pattern of activities and interests. Earlier in the year, following a survey of all Kendal residents, there was finally a decision to adopt formal names for each of the eight ponds on the campus. Respondents were asked to choose among three systems for naming them: after Quaker colleges, after flora and fauna, or after their physical features. They chose the third option, resulting in the following designations:

- Big Rock Pond (adjacent to the Phase II cottages), now referred to simply as "Rock Pond"
- Center Pond (in front of the Heiser Community Center)
- Farmer's Pond (named for "Farmer Joe," who used to "fill his tractor with water from the pond with an old can that finally disappeared from sight a couple of years ago.")
- Island Pond (opposite parking lot 7)
- Woodland Pond (opposite lot 10, in the woods), sometimes known as "Hidden Pond"
- Green Pond (accessible via "Hallie's Alley")

Staff members Maggie Stark (left) and Anne Cunningham with the time capsule that was buried on the Kendal campus in 2000.

- Meadow Pond (adjacent to Phase I cottages)

More recently the campus has gained two more bodies of water. One is Buttonbush Pond, just inside the perimeter road next to the apartments, formerly a marsh area that can now hold water for most of the year. The other, known informally as Triangle Pond, emerged during construction of the cottages in Phase III.

May of 1998 saw the first formal recognition that many new residents would no longer be individuals who had been in communication with the founding planners before Kendal opened, but rather had initiated contact a year or two later. Recognition came in the form of a "newcomers club," made up of residents who had moved in within the prior year. The Hospitality Committee organized a dinner for the new arrivals in the private dining room in the Fox & Fell so they could get to know each other better and could share information as needed. Committee leaders Dot Holbrook and Esther Hunt found that the newcomers were unanimous in hoping that events such as this would continue in future years. By 2000, their expectation was fulfilled, though in an unusual fashion, when a newcomers club was "established" anew. The function continues until this writing, though without any additional reincarnations.

The arrival of the new millennium also inspired residents and staff to create a "time capsule" of information that might be of interest to their successors. At the annual Kendal at Oberlin "CommUnity Picnic" on June 22, 2000, the capsule was buried with a full complement of poems, circulars, photographs, publications, newspaper and magazine articles, financial statements, and a mix of other materials.

Narrowcast News

Internal communication on the Kendal campus in its early years was handled primarily through *The Kendalight*, the monthly newsletter distributed to all residents, and posters and other notices on bulletin boards. This worked well, though it didn't accommodate short-notice events or changes in scheduling that arose too late to be included in *The Kendalight*'s month-long calendar. By winter of 2000-01, a solution was in view: "Channel 19," an in-house, closed-circuit television station that could continuously display calendar information and other notices on television sets in cottages and apartments. At any time of day or night, residents could receive updated information. The major challenge was how to get this information into the right format for transmission over the television circuit.

The solution to this challenge required an impressive feat of design and engineering known as the "whirligig." The reader will find that dictionaries define a whirligig as "a child's toy having a whirling motion, or a merry-go-round." The second definition was more appropriate (see chapter VI for a more detailed description of the device). The mechanism was quite remarkable, and it almost always worked, though the resulting on-screen images were occasionally less readable than many liked due to the inconsistency of the design and production of the one-page notices. In the May 2001 *Kendalight*, the Ad Hoc TV committee passed along some suggestions for those submitting pages for Channel 19:

> "A 1¼ inch margin on ALL sides is necessary for inclusion of the whole page on the screen… Remember to use type large enough to be read on a small TV screen… Try to use color…"

The "whirligig" was a hit, but before long the specter of technological change was looming. In August 2001, Ad Hoc TV Committee chair Bill Hayward informed KORA that a computerized

Above: Resident Bill DeWitt with the "whirligig," the device he and others designed and built to display information to be shared over Channel 19.

Opposite page: A close-up of the whirligig"s mechanism, featuring a turn-table and places for more than a dozen announcements.

The KORA Food Committee is one of three resident groups focused on topics of nutrition and food selection. Here members of the committee staffed a table at an early activities fair. From left were Eileen Dettman, David Evans, Henry Cady, and Elizabeth Runyan, joined by Chef Loren, who was Kendal at Oberlin's chef at the time.

version of Channel 19 was coming, a change that would require "computer literate residents" to operate the system. The transition took longer than expected. The computerized version of Channel 19 was not in operation until October 2002, but the change has proved its value to the community. The mechanical turntable took its place in storage, and recent attempts to locate any pieces of it have yielded only a few photographs. Meanwhile, the computerized version is on its third generation of software and continues to adapt to evolving needs and opportunities.

You Are What You Eat

In keeping with Kendal's emphasis on wellness, residents have traditionally encouraged measures to promote healthy food choices in the dining areas. The balance between flavor and the advantages of a low-sodium diet is a regular topic of discussion on the campus.

Presaging later and more extensive measures to promote healthy eating, the July 1999 issue of *The Kendalight* announced a pioneering new policy for the Langston Express:

> "The selections on the salad bar in the Langston Express have expanded and taken on a different look with new containers. Items served in the red containers are the heart-healthy choices that are less than 30% calories from fat…."

Illustrating that progress often comes in the form of two steps forward and one backward, the same issue of *The Kendalight* also announced "freshly baked bagels" in the deli section. More recently, Kendal at Oberlin has led the way among Kendal affiliates in the effort to reduce or eliminate trans-fats in diets.

Residents' interest in healthy eating has continued unabated, as evidenced by the proliferation of committees devoted to the topic (discussed elsewhere in this history). An important advance has been the addition of detailed nutritional information in the daily menus posted in the dining areas and, more recently, on the KORA web site. Nutritional information had always been included in the Kendal system's food data base, but its inclusion on printed and web-cast menus has required the system to reformulate data to reflect local preferences such as low-sodium content.

The Matter of Growth

During 1998, five years after the opening of the community, the Kendal at Oberlin board gave some thought to the possibility of expansion. Demand for cottages and apartments had been strong and, with the benefit of five years of experience, the programs and systems that had been so carefully designed by the planners

Demmie and Jep Carrell (left), shown with fellow residents Nan and Dick Ninde, whose extraordinary generosity in 2002 made possible the creation of the Ninde Scholars Program, which provides funding to help all students at Oberlin High School attend college. The program offers tutoring and college preparation services, including assisting students to find scholarships and other forms of financial aid.

were proving their worth. At the March 19, 1998, KORA Council meeting, trustee Dorothy Luciano—who was also a Kendal resident—used carefully qualified language in a report on this topic, as quoted on the opening page of this chapter. It was clear that Kendal residents enjoyed the culture and scale of the community as it was, and the trustees understood that there might be concern about growth.

The tentative and cautionary note in Luciano's report was warranted. Less than a year later, in February 1999, after extensive discussion among the members of the board and with others, trustee and resident Sadie Taylor delivered the following statement, again to the KORA Council:

Resident Bill Hayward, who brought to Kendal a long career in communications work, including broadcasting, shown recording one of his many public service announcements for replay on radio. His series in the 1990s included "Speaking from Oberlin" and "Senior Focus."

> "[The] growth focus group concluded that consideration of expansion for us similar to that of Crosslands and Longwood (Cartmel and Coniston) is not appropriate now. It will be reviewed in the future."

Discussion had focused on creating a new, additional living area on or adjacent to the Kendal campus, with accommodations similar to those offered in the cottages that had been built in 1993. The expanded area would have its own special appearance, however, rather than attempting to duplicate the "classic" units. But conditions did not yet seem ripe for expansion, and the board members reluctantly put aside their aspirations.

The topic did not die away, however, and a few years later there was again active discussion of a plan for expansion, once more drawing mixed reviews from residents. While recognizing the need for some additional space, many were concerned by the suggestion by Richard J. Dunn, then chair of the Kendal Board of Directors, that "the generation of residents emerging toward the end of the coming decade will bring with them lifestyles significantly different than those of our founding residents."[16] Current residents noted that many of them had chosen Kendal precisely because it was smaller than other comparable retirement communities, and that they did not want to lose any of the undeveloped spaces on the campus.[17]

Later in 2002, following extensive discussion of the issues raised by residents concerning the "growth initiative," Dunn again wrote to residents on the matter. His approach was somewhat different this time:

> "Concerning the Growth Initiative, if we could start over again, I never would have favored the use of the word 'growth.' What appeared to be a harmless, descriptive word to the board has proven to be a red flag to many residents. We probably should have anticipated that but did not."[18]

Planning for expansion continued in the coming months, but with more emphasis on issues of environment and sustainability that had surfaced in talks with residents and others. Notes prepared for a June 2003 charrette session by the architectural firm of Herman Gibans Fodor identified those issues:

- Energy efficiency
- Renewable energy sources
- Environmentally preferable building materials
- Water conservation
- Recycling
- Waste management

In addition to these environmental concerns, the expansion project also aimed to "improve the quality of resident life" and "assure the financial success of Kendal at Oberlin," among other goals. Less clearly articulated but ever present in the planning process was the desire that some prospective residents had voiced for somewhat larger cottages, with higher ceilings and more window area.

Several weeks later, the subsequent discussion of issues and objectives concentrated on more specific topics:

- Independent living cottages: Residents thought new cottages should be larger than the existing ("classic") units, but smaller than comparable facilities available in other communities. Their concerns focused on overly large units lingering as empty "white elephants."

- Assisted living units: There was support for the recommended increase in the number of assisted living units given the plans to add 36 more independent living cottages. They felt that flexibility in design would be important, including the potential to join two adjacent rooms. Finally, they wanted to make sure to protect beloved existing exterior views and develop a "country kitchen"

Above: Kendal residents and Oberlin College alumnae Eileen Dettman (left) and Jane Hannauer, both accomplished musicians, shown at the Oberlin Conservatory of Music, where they visit often.

Opposite page: Kendal residents serving as volunteers at the Oberlin Heritage Center, shown here in front of Monroe House, one of OHC's three historic buildings available for touring.

area to be shared by residents and staff requiring space or equipment beyond that available in their living units.

- Dining spaces: Residents felt it was important to maintain flexible seating, but also to add more seating for new residents if the community were to grow. They also urged improved acoustics in both the Fox and Fell and Langston dining areas.

- Heiser Community Center: There was strong support for enlarging the child-care facility and relocating the marketing and admissions office to a more central and visible place on the campus.[19]

The question of where to add the new independent living cottages on the campus was a hot-button issue. There was near-unanimity that they should not be part of an "in-fill" strategy, i.e., scattered among existing cottages, for fear that this arrangement would interfere with exterior views. They preferred a site to the west of the perimeter road, across the road from parking lots one through three. This is precisely where the second and third clusters of new cottages would ultimately be developed, the first cluster being located south of the perimeter road, across from

Buttonbush Pond. These new cottages, known as Phases I, II, and III, are not only larger than the "classic" units, but also located further away from the center of the campus. Covered walkways still link them to the Heiser Center, however, although in some cases this has involved considerable negotiation.

At the same time that the matter of expansion of the Kendal campus was being debated, another proposal for a new initiative was on the table as well. Initially titled "Kendal Continuing Care at Home," later shortened to "Kendal at Home," this program was designed as a coordinated system of services for older residents of the region who choose to remain in their homes rather than move to Kendal. This was an innovation for the entire Kendal system, but it would have no significant impact on the use of space on the current Kendal campus. If there were any concerns on the part of current residents, they were focused on the financial risks the new venture might pose for Kendal at Oberlin.

Above: The late resident Sara Balogh recording one of her many readings of books for the blind, a service for which she received wide notice.

Opposite page: Len Garver (left) and his fellow resident Ernie Eddy (background) worked in 1996 with members of a local Cub Scout troop on a project in the Kendal woodshop.

Above: A group of Kendal "Grandparent Readers" in 1996, shown with children from Eastwood Primary School in Oberlin. The program has been credited with helping the school's students improve their reading performance.

Residents Nina Love (left) and Gerlind Koerner (opposite page) shown reading with students at Eastwood School. The program is a favorite with residents and Eastwood's teachers and students alike.

About Town

An early concern among some residents of Oberlin, including a few key leaders of Oberlin College, was that introducing a retirement community could blur the image of a college town, affecting recruitment of both students and faculty. Those early fears have not materialized, and in fact Kendal and its residents devote a great deal of their time and energy to activities that benefit the town, both directly and indirectly. Some of these activities are profiled in chapter six of this history, "Our Favorite Things," while others are not as easily described in prose. Many of these

outreach efforts emerged in the early years of Kendal's operation, and by 2005 were already in full operation, such as:

- **Oberlin City Schools**. Kendal residents are generally interested in education at all levels, and are frequently found in the Oberlin City Schools working as volunteers and helping in other ways. Specific examples have included the "Listening Post" program, in which residents engaged informally in conversations with middle school students about whatever topics the students would like to discuss; the "Grandparent Readers" program, in which residents share books one-on-one with students at Eastwood Elementary School; and the "Publicity Plugs" program, which provides the schools with volunteer reporting, writing, and photography to prepare stories about the schools in area newspapers.

- **Oberlin College**. Many Kendal residents are OC alumni and retired faculty and staff, so their connections to the college are very close. Residents may audit OC courses without charge, and many regularly offer volunteer assistance in on-campus offices such as the Mudd Learning Center and the college's archives. Residents also serve regularly as mentors for OC students in courses where contact with an older generation is encouraged, and as hosts for college events such as reunions and first-year student orientation. In addition, residents predictably make up a good share of the audiences for many of the more than 400 concerts, recitals, lectures, and other performances that take place on the OC campus each year.

- **Oberlin Public Library**. Kendal residents are active users of the library's holdings and services, and many have also served as volunteers.

- **Other area nonprofits**. Local churches, social service groups, and community action organizations are regular beneficiaries of the time, advice, and resources of Kendal residents. The Oberlin Heritage Center, for example, holds many of its events in Kendal facilities, and many Kendalites are members and leaders of the League of Women Voters. Management Assistance for Nonprofit Agencies (MANA), a volunteer management consulting group founded in 2003 by Kendal resident Don Illig. provides consulting advice and assistance to nonprofit organizations and governmental agencies in Lorain County, charging nothing but a nominal overhead fee to cover mileage, copying, etc.

- **Economic activity**. The presence of more than 300 seniors so close to the center of Oberlin represents a major market for shops, groceries, restaurants, and other local outlets. This is particularly important because OC students for the most part are away during the summer months, taking with them a significant share of demand for goods and services. The year-round presence of Kendal helps offset that summer drop-off. From a philanthropic perspective, the presence of Kendal's residents is an important asset to the community's nonprofit and public service organizations. A notable example was the generous gift by residents Dick and Nancy Ninde to create the Ninde Scholars Program, which supports efforts at Oberlin College and in the Oberlin Schools to help underrepresented and low-income students and those who would be the first in their families to attend college.

- **Regional outreach**. In addition to building mechanisms to promote interaction among residents, there were efforts early on to communicate with the larger region. In recent years this has taken the form of ads and public service announcements in major media, which serve to attract inquiries from potential residents. In the community's earlier years, the late resident Bill Hayward was a stalwart contributor to the public airwaves with two series of radio features, "Speaking from Kendal" and "Senior Focus." Drawing on his long experience in media, Hayward researched, wrote, and recorded short essays designed to provide useful information on topics ranging from "Growing Old Gracefully" to "When to Stop Driving."

Beyond these impacts, Kendal and the City of Oberlin negotiated a series of payments in lieu of taxes ("PILOT") when the community first opened. Much of Kendal's land and buildings are tax-exempt because of their use for health care-related purposes, though they still depend on the city for services such as police, fire, etc. The agreement helps the city continue to make those services available. Kendal also pays real estate taxes on a portion of its property.

Residents examining the merchandise at the 2012 plant sale in the Heiser Center included (from right) Janet Bolland, Marilyn Myerson, and Fran Cooper. The annual sale is organized by the Horticulture Committee.

Chapter V

Growing the Community (2006-12)

Special Sighting: The twelve tiny mallard ducklings (less than one day old, probably), who hatched under a bush in the Courtyard Garden and fell... into a drain in the lawn. They swam around there for hours until spotted by sharp-eyed Renee Watson, who works in the Stephens Care Center. She rescued them, using a long-handled net from the swimming pool. They were then ushered out of the garden, through the corridor, and into the outdoors by Bill Schreiner and their mother.

Betty Weinstock in her "Nature Sightings" column in *The Kendalight*, May 2011

MANAGEMENT THEORISTS like to note that organizations have life-cycles, with various stages of development such as embryonic, growth, etc. This concept of the evolution of an organization assumes that at some point it will enter a "mature" phase, suggesting that it has stopped growing and is more focused on sustaining its existence than on new ventures. Kendal at Oberlin does not yet seem to have reached a "mature" stage of development, and it has already begun generating new initiatives.

Status Quo Ante

Kendal entered this phase of its life at the age of 13, a good indication of its continuing newness, although in this case it wasn't an issue of hormones. The community had successfully opened and operated at capacity for more than a decade, winning good marks from residents and reviewers alike. It was in sound financial con-

Above: If there's anything more inspiring than the children in Kendal's Early Learning Center, we don't know about it. Here a group of KELC kids belted out a number in their 2013 Valentine's Day production.

Below: Ira Steinberg (at left), one of several volunteers from Kendal who help local area residents with their tax returns in the AARP Tax Advisors Program, shown here working with a couple at the Oberlin Senior Center.

dition, riding the longest peacetime period of economic growth in the country's history, including a dramatic increase in the value of housing. Inflation had been low since the early 1980s, setting the stage for rapid economic expansion. This made it relatively easy for prospective residents to move to Kendal, since their prior homes were selling quickly and bringing record prices. Forecast for the years ahead was an echo of the "Baby Boom," as the generation born between 1946 and 1964 was about to begin its entry into retirement, bringing with it what was expected to be another surge in demand for the kind of environment Kendal offers.

As exciting as the future looked, it would bring some challenges as well. Perhaps most fundamental was an intensification of the recognition in the late 1990s and early 2000s that Kendal's new and prospective residents were increasingly unknown to the individuals who had carried out the early planning for the community, and that they did not necessarily share the same life experiences that had so deeply influenced the "Founders." Would they subscribe to the same values and traditions that were central to the community's early success?

Overshadowing even that challenge, however, was another that would affect individual residents—continuing and new—as well as the overall community: the extended period of fiscal and economic stress that observers have called the "Great Recession." The recession is generally seen as a result of the housing "bubble" and related financial instruments, such as mortgage-backed securities, affecting virtually every aspect of the economy both in the U.S. and worldwide. Economists consider the recession to have lasted for six quarters, beginning in December 2007 and ending in June 2009. Five of those six quarters yielded declines in the country's Gross Domestic Product (GDP), a measure of the value of all the goods and services produced in the nation. Unemployment rose to near-record levels, housing prices fell sharply, and investment markets sagged.[20] American families, now more dependent than ever before on market-sensitive resources such as 401K and 403b accounts and other "defined contribution" plans to support themselves after their careers ended, looked forward to retirement with less confidence than they had earlier – and with considerably less equity in their residences. While the recession technically ended in June 2009, economic growth and employment have continued to be sluggish even as productivity has increased dramatically. In December 2012, wry observers directed "happy fifth birthday" greetings toward the recession that had supposedly ended thirty months earlier.

Planning as Part of Leadership

In 2006, however, there was little evidence of this approaching storm. The nation's GDP was growing, consumer spending was high, and markets were for the most part strong – though increasingly dominated by instruments so complex and risky that few investors were able to determine their real value. The most dramatic shock to the nation's momentum had been the terrorist attacks on U.S. soil on September 11, 2001, but in many ways the economy had found ways to rebound in the years following even such horrific events.

At Kendal, the view was positive and the prospects for the years ahead looked rosy. In a joint statement in the "Disclosure Statement" published in May 2007 to report on 2006 outcomes and to advise current and prospective residents about future trends, Kendal's board chair and its CEO wrote:

> "2006 was an action-packed year full of evidence of a strong future for those we serve. The year included a mosaic of diverse events and actions including strong financial performance, full census in our current residential units and the successful completion of our new cottage units."[21]

The statement went on to describe completion of the first elements in a ten-year plan for Kendal's development, including new meeting and conference room spaces, a new nursing care wing, and "Phase I," twelve new independent living cottages. These new cottages were the first of three clusters of units with updated design and larger floor space than found in the older, "classic" cottages built in 1993. A wetland restoration project in the pond

Residents and community members participating in a Tai Chi class offered regularly in the Kendal Fitness Center. Swimming and fitness classes are open to area residents on a fee basis, space permitting.

in front of the Heiser Center was also completed, resulting in a larger water area and more native plant species. Further down in the statement, however, came recognition that it was important to remain alert:

> "Kendal at Oberlin's Board and management continue to scan the environment and are ever-conscious of changes in the market or other developments to which we need to respond... We believe that diligence and vigilance... and willingness to make appropriate adjustments are critical to accomplishing our mission."[22]

This spirit of cautious adventure was also reflected in changes in the organizational structure for Kendal. Recognizing that some prospective residents were considering remaining in their homes rather than moving to retirement communities, Kendal at Home

Above: View of Phase II cottages, which opened in 2009. They are built along the edge of Rock Pond. (Photo copyright William H. Webb)

Opposite page: Stephens Care Center staff member Laura Auble and resident Ruth Schwaegerle jointly cut the ribbon to mark the opening of the expanded assisted living facilities in the Whittier Wing in 2012.

had been created in 2004 to offer a package of services and assistance to members who live in the larger region but choose not to move to the campus in Oberlin. Established as a nonprofit organization and financed in part through a start-up loan from Kendal at Oberlin, Kendal at Home focuses on health and wellness, social interactions, and home maintenance support for its members. In addition, a new entity called Kendal Northern Ohio was created as a supporting organization for both Kendal at Oberlin and Kendal at Home. This pattern of reaching new markets with new services has continued with the addition in 2009 of a partnership between Kendal Northern Ohio and Senior Independence, an Ohio-based provider of home health care with more than 30 years experience. This partnership now offers home health and related services to

clients living at Kendal at Oberlin, to participants in Kendal at Home, and to other people living independently in the region.

Given the success of the Phase I development that was completed in 2006, Kendal proceeded to build and offer the remaining two clusters of new cottages envisioned in the planning process. Phase II opened in 2009, and Phase III in 2011.

In the course of a few years, the corporate and program structure for Kendal's presence in the region had grown much more complex, and its reach had extended to previously unserved populations. These decisions, some of which are still playing out, were reached as part of an intensive and continuing planning function led by Kendal at Oberlin's board and management, with participation by its residents. The role of residents in these discussions

Above: The groundbreaking ceremony for Kendal's Phase I cottages—the first new residences built since 1993—drew a large crowd of prospective residents. After the cottages opened in 2006, Ed Wardwell (far left) and his wife Anne moved in, as did Del and Betty Jenkins (far right).

Opposite page: View of the bridge built across Buttonbush Pond to provide a covered walkway for Phase I residents heading for the Heiser Center.

has grown over time, reflecting some of the concerns raised in the 2002-03 interplay concerning the board's "growth initiative." This approach has guided decision-making for Kendal at Oberlin as the "Great Recession" has arrived—and lingered.

New Times, New Methods

Recognizing the intersecting effects of market behavior and financial planning, Kendal has formally integrated forecasts of market demand into its strategic and tactical decisions about pricing, facilities planning, and services. The most easily seen illustrations of this phenomenon occur in the admission process, where the organization helps prospective residents progress through the various stages of interest in Kendal. In 2012, for example, as ele-

CHAPTER V: GROWING THE COMMUNITY 93

ments of the "Great Recession" lingered and depressed housing markets nationwide continued to complicate decisions by potential residents, applicants who had made the decision to place themselves on the Kendal "priority list" were offered an opportunity to take advantage of a discount in the entrance fee for a limited period. This was an unusual approach, and the decision to proceed with it involved careful deliberations that involved Kendal's board, management, and residents to ensure that all elements of the community were aware and supportive. The strategy was effective, resulting in a significant uptick in commitments from prospective residents that are intended to help move Kendal at Oberlin's occupancy rate back up into the low to mid-90 percent range where it had hovered for much of the community's pre-recession existence.

The admission process has also adapted to changes in the use of information technology by prospective residents. Not only do most seniors examining options for continuing care communities "visit" Kendal first via the Worldwide Web, they are also increasingly engaged with social media such as Facebook, Twitter, and others. Beginning in 2011, Kendal has built a presence both on the web and in social media to supplement its traditional communication programs, with current residents volunteering content for the postings. This is a marked change from the prior pattern, in which the most effective ways of reaching prospective residents included small ads in *The New Yorker* and spots on fine arts and public radio stations in the region. While those approaches continue, it is clear that Kendal's future residents are more and more comfortable with evolving communication media.

Policy Shifts

While the diversity of topics that dominate conversations among Kendal residents is not very different from that found in cities and suburbs elsewhere, it is the matter of health care that drives most

The courtyard created by the addition of the swimming pool and the fitness center has been beautified with walkways, a gazebo, and an explosion of plants. (Photo courtesy of Bill Schreiner)

residents to consider and select a continuing care retirement community as a place to live in their senior years. The concept of a CCRC is inherently reassuring: a full spectrum of care available within a single organization, with continuity among staff members, neighbors, and surroundings. The added commitment that no prudent Kendal resident will be required to leave the community for financial reasons is an important benefit.

For a half century, the U.S. has tried to confront twin dilemmas regarding health care: seemingly uncontrollable increases in its costs, and inequities in its availability to the entire population of the country. With the introduction of Medicare and Medicaid in the 1960s, the nation made major progress in extending health care to the elderly and to the needy, but the country's heavy reliance on employer-sponsored health care plans left many "working poor" uncovered. At the same time, advances in medical science and in biomedical technology, while promising more effective approaches to diagnosis and treatment, were also pushing up the costs of health at rates far above other standard measures of inflation. The Affordable Care Act, enacted in 2010 and called "Obamacare" in the 2012 presidential campaign, addresses some of these issues by putting in place mechanisms to extend health care coverage to millions of individuals who were previously uncovered. It does not, however, take direct action to control the rising costs of health care, instead focusing on preventive care and other measures with long-term benefits, including lower costs.

Kendal's planning approach has integrated what is known about the implementation of the Affordable Care Act into its calculations, although much of the bill's impact won't take effect until 2014. For much of 2012 and continuing into 2013, the administration and a committee of residents and board members labored to develop a relationship with one or more health care systems that will provide flexibility and access to additional resources to accommodate the evolving landscape of health care policy. The approach being pursued assumes that the existing pattern of physician coverage supplemented by the presence of one or two active, experienced nurse practitioners will be continued. Forming a partnership with one or more larger health care systems will give Kendal residents access to additional coverage as needed.

In a presentation[23] to residents in January 2013, chief health services officer Stacy Terrell outlined the strategy's objectives:

- Advancement of "slow medicine," an approach to diagnosis and treatment advocated by, among others, Dr. Dennis McCullough of Dartmouth College's medical school, in which the practitioner listens closely to the patient and evaluates all aspects of his or her environment.

- Focus on wellness and prevention, evidenced-based care paths, quality of care, and minimizing hospital admissions and readmissions.
- Preparation for the Accountable Care Organizations.
- Move to a staffing model calling for one physician and two full time nurse practitioners.
- Intensify Kendal's emphasis on learning.
- Explore other creative ideas, e.g., a geriatric clinic, integration of home health and Kendal's Health and Wellness Clinic, and partnerships with other senior care providers.

Residential Units, Kendal at Oberlin (May 2013)

Type of Unit	Apts.	Cotts.	Total
Studio	4	9	13
One-bedroom	17	29	46
One-bedroom deluxe	0	1	1
New one-bedroom	0	4	4
One-bedroom den	18	32	50
One-bedroom den deluxe	0	6	6
New one-bedroom den	0	10	10
Two-bedroom	7	24	31
Two-bedroom deluxe	0	1	1
New two-bedroom	0	12	12
Two-bedroom den	2	33	35
Two-bedroom den deluxe	0	4	4
New two-bedroom den	0	6	6
New two-bedroom den deluxe	0	4	4
Total	48	175	223

The late Kendal residents Paul and Sally Arnold shared a bicycle ride across Oberlin's Tappan Square on a chilly fall day. Paul was a distinguished professor of art and a print maker at Oberlin College for many years, and Sally was an active member of the community.

Chapter VI

Our Favorite Things

As part of the process of researching and writing this history, residents were asked to identify places, programs, and other features of Kendal that seemed particularly important to them. Many are profiled below, while others—no less important—do not lend themselves to traditional program descriptions. These latter items have engendered warm responses, such as the following:

- "The staff—top to bottom—who are unfailingly polite, concerned, and helpful…"
- "Kendal at Oberlin is unique! It's friendly, vibrant, creative…, with residents with outstanding talents…"
- "I no longer need to cook main meals!"
- "The fact that Kendal is within walking distance of the town square means that residents can be part of the community and Oberlin College activities – concerts, lectures, parades, etc…"
- "Beautiful flower arrangements every day!"
- "Diversity of interesting residents with lifetimes of service to society…"
- "So many backgrounds, vocations and avocations. Getting to know people is so interesting."
- "The generous, supportive spirit of this Kendal…"

Among the features lending themselves to prose descriptions are those described below. Some of the information provided here was drawn from material submitted by residents involved in these activities, in many cases as part of the collection of overviews gathered by Robert Taylor for Kendal's 15th anniversary celebration in 2008.

Above: During 2013 the Art Committee organized two consecutive retrospective shows of the work of the late resident Paul Arnold in the Kendal Gallery. With help from the Arnold family, they were able to bring in pieces owned by residents and other friends and admirers of Arnold's work.

Left: One of the entries in Kendal's 2012 show featuring banner art done by students at Oberlin High School. The students were asked to adopt the styles and methods of various famous artists in executing the banners, and to offer written descriptions of the artists' approaches on cards accompanying their entries.

Art

Even occasional visitors to Kendal quickly sense that art in all its varieties is a major interest. Kendal provides three galleries where art can be displayed: the Kendal Gallery, the Friends Gallery, and the Community Art Walls. Exhibits are on view throughout the

Kendal's residents include several quilters, three of whom were featured in a show in the Kendal Gallery during 2011. Above are fabric works by Peg Schultz (left) and Nancy Garver. The third quilter was Polly Carroll.

year in all three galleries, usually including receptions with presentations by the artists whose work is being shown. In addition, residents and others have contributed or loaned works of art to Kendal over its lifetime, many of which are permanently displayed elsewhere in the dining areas, halls, and corridors of the public spaces. Kendal also hosts two rotating art shows in alternating years, "Kendal Creates" and "Kendal Collects," featuring works produced or owned, respectively, by Kendal residents. Works shown include both two- and three-dimensional items, and it is a sign of the depth of the talent and the collections of residents that content is seldom repeated in later years.

One of Kendal's longest-standing groups, the Art Committee, coordinates these activities. Residents Nancy Gage and Louise

Richards were the first chairs of the committee, starting by focusing on donated works—befitting the group's origins as a spin-off from the House Committee. The late Paul Arnold, long-time Oberlin College art professor and print-maker, was for many years an anchor of the committee. In addition, the late resident Duncan Love developed a computerized archive of the 400 or so works contributed or loaned by residents, a system that is being continued by committee members Arn and Beth Lewis.

Audio Announcements

Responding to the needs of residents with limited vision, audio announcements were started in 2003. Kendal's resident-operated information stream, Channel 19, was up and running, but people with low vision could not see the announcements. Resident Connie Bimber asked KORA Council to purchase an answering machine to record menus and announcements for the next day or

Volunteers in the Audio Announcements group gathered in 2012 to celebrate the long-running program. Attending were (front row) Ann Potter and Lois Sook, and (back row) Donna Baznik, Jane Eddy, Connie Bimber (who coordinates the program), Terry Carlton, and June Swartwout.

two. While they are primarily for people with low vision, anyone can dial 440-774-9868 to hear the announcements.

Bimber recruited and trained 14 residents—two for each day of the week—and the first recording was made on March 31, 2003. It was soon clear that it was easier to remember to do the recording if assignments came around once a week rather than every other week. As some readers found they couldn't continue, the group contracted to seven regular recorders and two substitutes, but some members of the original crew from 2003 are still engaged.

Cardinal Shop

Before residents had been at Kendal for six months, there was a committee at work planning a gift shop. In the March 10, 1994, issue of *The Kendalight*, a message from Gift Shop Committee chair Ruth Hansen reported, "The Gift Shop plans are going ahead, but until we have final plans for storage space, display cases and other necessities, we can't make any definite dates for our 'Grand Opening.' All of you, founders, staff and employees, can be a big help if you will take a few minutes to make a list of articles you would like to have available in your gift shop…" The project was under way.

Within two months, the facility took on the name "The Cardinal Shoppe" (that final "pe" was dropped quickly) and acquired shelving and other furniture from a local pharmacy that was relocating. Over the years its inventory has adapted to the needs and interests of residents and their families and guests, incorporating not only traditional items found in such outlets but also crafts made by residents themselves.

Ceramics/Pottery Group

Creative activities director Michele Tarsitano-Amato has periodically led pottery projects, focusing on low-fire ceramics, for residents of the Stephens Care Center. For independent living residents, resident Joyce Parker began leading a limited program of clay workshops in 2009, soon after she moved to Kendal. This program brings shipments of stoneware clay to Kendal twice a year, which is then used for "hand building" projects that are fired as guest pieces in a kiln at the Oberlin College Pottery Co-op. These workshops take place either in the Horticulture/Art Room or in an open carport space. The mid-range glazing on the pieces that emerge from these workshops make them a particular source of pleasure to their creators.

In both formats, the ceramics and pottery activities offered at Kendal often represent residents' first exposure to the art form, but it is seldom their last.

Channel 19

Among the most visible approaches to disseminating information to the Kendal community is Channel 19, the closed-circuit television channel operated by and for residents, accessible via the cable TV in all units on the campus.

The method used to generate and disseminate daily announcements has changed markedly since the early years here. The system began as one-page calendars posted weekly on the main bulletin board, the Stephens Care Center bulletin board, and in the library. Mary Louise VanDyke launched the process and passed it on to Betty Verlie. Don VanDyke enlarged the pages and posted them each Sunday morning.

Technology intervened, however, and in 2001 residents began producing a series of slides for closed-circuit TV (channel 19) using a device featuring a large wooden turntable that rotated on its axis while a video camera photographed the slides. The "whirligig" was designed and built by a team of residents including Bill DeWitt, Len Garver, and Len Singer. The calendar pages and posters for individual events were inserted in the appropriate slot on the device. It was complicated and labor-intensive, but it worked.

In 2002 the "whirligig" was replaced by more modern technology, a computer program that generates video images for the television channel. A team of residents still takes individual days of the week to prepare slides, but now they work entirely on the computer, using software to format the information. The "whirligig" is gone, but it is fondly remembered.

Community Gardens

While many residents cultivate gardens around their cottages or in the area outside their first-floor apartments, some have grander aspirations. For them the community gardens, located at the southern edge of the campus next to the tennis courts, offer access to sunny plots of soil that they can reserve for their efforts. The area is fenced to protect it from incursions from visiting livestock, and advice for novice gardeners is available from more experienced neighbors working on adjacent plots.

Courtyard Garden

The courtyard adjacent to the Stephens Care Center that today features a garden and walkways was not envisioned in the original plan for the campus. As noted elsewhere in this history, the swimming pool that with its hallway encloses the courtyard was not built until 1996, after extensive debate about how large a pool would be needed. The KORA Horticulture Committee became the principal arena for planning for the new garden.

In addition to plantings, the plan for the garden called for a gazebo and a sun-filled entranceway into the care center.

A rose in the courtyard garden between the assisted living area and the fitness center. (Photo courtesy of Bill Schreiner)

The Woodshop crew assembled the gazebo, while a commercial contractor installed the entryway. The initial surface of the walkway areas was flagstones, but this was replaced with a smoother surface several years later to make it easier for wheelchairs and walkers to get around. Resident Bill Schreiner has tended the courtyard for more than a decade.

The garden is used by residents and visitors associated with all areas of Kendal, from the population of the adjoining Stephens Care Center to the children of Kendal's Early Learning Center, for whom it is a trip into a floral fantasy land.

Eureka!

Many visitors and friends of Kendal are pleasantly surprised to learn that the community produces a thriving literary magazine. The first issue of *Eureka!* was published in May 2004, and subsequent issues have appeared three times a year since then. Original articles and illustrations are solicited by the editors from their fellow residents, and occasionally from non-residents. A particularly helpful local printer helps assemble and produce the magazine within the budget allotted by the residents association.

The idea for the magazine was proposed by resident Ben Lenz, and fellow resident Nancy Hultquist agreed to serve as its first coordinator (in reality its editor), working with a board of twelve residents. After five years she was succeeded by Robert Taylor. A contest to name the new publication produced "Eureka!," and the project was off and running. Copies of the printed magazine are sent without charge to all Kendal residents.

106   HISTORY OF KENDAL AT OBERLIN

There are several traditions associated with *Eureka!*, including a dinner meeting for all contributors and board members as each issue is published. Another is a set of wooden letters (spelling E-U-R-E-K-A-!), produced by Ben Lenz, that rotate among editorial board members who host each of the dinners. The letters are accompanied by a small toy bathtub, evoking Archimedes and his discovery of the principle that is named for him, at which point he is said to have declared "Eureka!" in celebration.

Exercise Group (Strengthening/Stretching)

In 1995 the late resident Barbara Leonard organized this group, leading the exercises from the auditorium stage. Two years later the late Mary Emma Walker, with advice from former Kendal staff members Kevin Meyer and Kimberly Cardinal, created an exercise audio tape, still in use twice a week. For the third weekly session the group uses a variety of exercise video tapes.

This history can do no better than to reprint excerpts from a poem written in 2006 by current resident Thelma Morris that appeared in the 2008 "Historical Potpourri" assembled by resident Robert Taylor to celebrate Kendal's 15th anniversary:

> Mary Emma's voice breaks through morning reveries
>   as we gather in the meeting room, and move
>   in sync with exercise routines she once recorded.
>   We are guided firmly through arm stretches, leg lifts, all
>   suited to sedentary seniors eager to be fit.
>   Everyone is earnest, intent on following the directions.
> After fifty energetic minutes,
>   she instructs us to be seated, close our eyes.
>   Her voice grows soft as she tells us to breathe deeply…
>   exhaling longer than our inhaled breath. Sensations of
>   serenity spread from head to neck, to shoulders… arms…
>   trunk, knees and toes…..
> Good morning, good morning, Mary Emma.

The Fleet

Tucked into and behind garages and carports across the campus are a number of canoes that represent Kendal's "fleet," dating back to the arrival of Ben and Pam Lenz in 2002 with their often-patched canoe. They were soon followed by Milton and Margaret-Ann Ellis with their canoe. A photo of the Ellises canoeing on Rock Pond, with their dog Toby aboard, became a standard illustration in Kendal literature.

Other canoeists followed: Jay and Fern Ingersoll in 2005 and Ed and Anne Wardwell in 2006. Don and Joyce Parker arrived in 2008 with a 17-foot canoe, trading down to a 14-footer to fit on their car. More recent arrivals in 2011 include Dan Reiber, a sail-canoe enthusiast, and Bud Spierling and Pauline Handman, who arrived without a canoe but bought the Ingersolls'. The group's outings have included Old Woman Creek in Huron, Findley Lake, the Vermilion River, the Black River, and Hinckley Lake.

Part of "the fleet" has also been pressed into duty on Center Pond, in front of Heiser Community Center. The late resident Bob Smith, an expert in electronics, launched his remote control miniature boat in the pond, only to have it run aground on a sand

Margaret-Ann and Milt Ellis in their canoe, with their dog Toby, navigating one of Kendal's ponds. (Photo by Bill Pappas Photography)

Max and Muriel Morgan, decorated for the occasion, as they headed out for the parade around Heiser Circle to celebrate Independence Day in 2011. Following along behind them were George and Ruth Bent.

bar. The Ellises were summoned to put their canoe in the water to rescue the stranded boat, but they also were caught on the sand bar. A lifeline thrown from the shore rescued them.

Fourth of July Program

The origin of this now annual event was best described by the late resident Katherine Prescott in 2008:

> "A group of us were having dinner about a week before the Fourth of July, 1994. Someone remarked that it was too bad that the Kendal agenda did not include any celebration of Independence Day. The result of that conversation was that Ann Burton more or less dared Clara Lucioli to organize a parade. So she did."

As Kay Prescott recalled the event, Kendal residents costumed themselves "fancifully" on the morning of July 4 to march around Heiser Circle, led by the late Doris Sable with her large U.S. flag. Audio came from tape-recorded music provided by Don VanDyke and from noise-makers wielded by residents. Stephens Care Center residents wore festive hats and rode in wheelchairs decorated specially for the fifteen-minute parade. As noted by current Independence Day chair Jim Helm, Kendal's first celebration of the nation's independence from England was thus organized by a native of England.

The celebration of Independence Day has become a regular fixture in the Kendal calendar, though the scale has grown. In addition to the parade around Heiser Circle, now larger and led by a fife and drum corps with a set of flag bearers and a stand-in for the Liberty Bell, there is a picnic lunch and a program in the auditorium, written in recent years by resident Robert Taylor, that features music and readings from American history.

Fun Fitness Week

In 2006 a relative of the late resident Mary Funkhouser described a "senior Olympics" event held annually at another retirement community. The KORA Fitness Committee chair, Jerry Berner, and creative activities director Michele Tarsitano-Amato took to it immediately. They modified it to include staff with residents and, emphasizing participation rather than performance, decided not to give out medals.

Kendal's first Fun Fitness Week was in September 2006, with nine events that attracted 84 residents and 38 staff. Fun Fitness Week has taken place every June since then. The 2013 edition, featuring 22 events, had 231 participants, including 149 residents, 64 administrators and staff members, and four guests. In addition, about 14 children and staff from Kendal's Early Learning Center participated in selected events. Events held every year in-

Residents Torie Young (left) and Joanne Norenberg playing miniature golf during Fun Fitness Week in 2011. (Photo by Eleanor Helper)

clude: bowling, observation walk, community walk, brain teasers, walking relay race, silly obstacle course, miniature golf, basketball, cycling, lap swim/water walking, and tennis court fun.

Geese

Perhaps not universally loved but certainly a popular topic of discussion, the annual—and increasingly year-round—presence of Canada geese is a prominent feature of the Kendal campus. Several of the ponds on the campus are favorite roosting areas, with new broods of goslings being hatched each spring. Gardeners dread their arrival, as do walkers who must deal with droppings that appear on walkways. As a result, there are periodic contro-

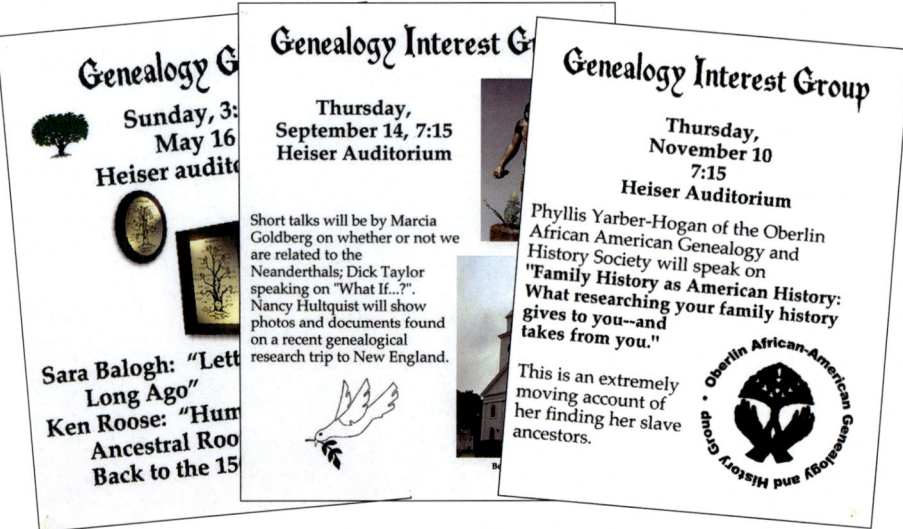

Samples of posters for sessions of the Genealogy Interest Group over the past decade, featuring presentations by Kendal at Oberlin residents as well as guest speakers from the region.

versies over whether the geese should be protected and nurtured, or should be shown the door. As this is written, current policy leans toward "management" of the situation.

Genealogy Interest Group

At Kendal, as elsewhere throughout the country and in many other parts of the world, engagement in genealogical research has exploded in recent decades. When Don and Nancy Hultquist moved to Kendal in 2002, they wrote to other residents to propose creation of a "Genealogy Interest Group" to discuss and promote writing of family histories and memoirs.

Response from residents was strong, and over the past decade there have been nearly 100 presentations made by residents and outside speakers. Some have addressed topics within the broad field of genealogical research, while others have been personal stories built around ancestral portraits or other objects, family stories, and even DNA analyses. Among the most memorable meetings were a series of sessions on African-American family histories sponsored jointly with the Oberlin Afro-American Genealogy and History Group.

The Hultquists have led the genealogy group for most of its existence, with residents Gretchen Roose, Peggy Reid, and Marcia Goldberg providing guidance as well in recent years.

Hallie's Alley

Casual visitors may overlook the rustic bridge over a drainage ditch east of the perimeter road just north of Meadow Pond. It's the entry way to "Hallie's Alley," known originally as "Hallie's

Path into Hallie's Alley through a heavily wooded area of the campus, featuring colorful flowers. (Photo by James Helm)

Way," a path through the woods around Green Pond named for the late resident Hallie Laird, who died in spring 1994. Her husband, the late Bert Laird, was interested in developing a nature project in her memory.

The bridge was designed and built by Hallie's brother-in-law, the late Roy G. ("Dutch") Harley, former CEO of a large construction firm. Bert Laird supervised the entire project, with much of the remaining work being done by Kendal residents. The project was completed in summer 1994, and today the "alley" delights the inquisitive visitor with stunning flowers and a leafy, wooded canopy. Resident volunteers periodically refresh the wood chips that help keep the pathway suitable for walking.

Health Newsletter

The health newsletter, properly titled "Health and Wellness News Items," is published nine times a year by a group of Kendal at Oberlin residents. The group selects and abstracts articles from publications such as the *New England Journal of Medicine*, the *Harvard Health Letter*, *Consumer Reports*, *The New York Times*, and others that present updates on health topics of interest to residents. Distribution of the newsletter is in hard copy or, to those who prefer electronic transmission, by email or KORA web site. Residents Don and Nancy Hultquist serve as editor and producer, respectively. Nancy Beauchamp, Jerry Berner, Pam Lenz, Don Parker, Bud Spierling, and May Zitani participate in selecting, abstracting, editing, and distributing.

The publication began at Kendal on Hudson, and in 2009 residents at Kendal at Oberlin were granted permission to circulate copies here. A year later, the Oberlin group's offer to help generate and produce the newsletter was eagerly accepted. For several years, it was published as an effective and exciting collaborative effort between the two groups. Beginning in 2011, the newsletter was also distributed to residents at Kendal at Lexington. When

Members of the Horticulture Committee turned out in 2013 to put in a garden of native plants on the shore of Center Pond in celebration of Kendal's 20th anniversary. (Photo courtesy of Don and Joyce Parker)

the Hudson group encountered some health challenges, the work gradually shifted to the Oberlin group. Since 2012, the newsletter has been generated solely at Oberlin.

Horticulture

Given Kendal's location in an area that was once covered with trees, marshes, and farms, it should come as no surprise that many residents take a strong interest in nurturing and cultivating plants. The organized discussion of these topics is centered in the KORA Horticulture Committee, but a great deal of the activity takes place at the individual level as residents make decisions about how best to add plant life to their immediate surroundings. Even then, however, many residents seek advice from the committee or its members before proceeding.

A recitation of topics discussed at the August 1996 meeting of the Horticulture Committee will offer a sense of the range of topics in play: plantings around the main entrance to Kendal; large plants obscuring the view out the pool windows; request to contribute toward the cost of building a cabana near the tennis courts; problem of clumps of dirt being placed into the compost pile; planning for seeds and bulbs for the coming year's growing season; and plants to screen electrical vaults on the campus.

Trees on the campus carry identification markers so that residents as well as staff and visitors can familiarize themselves with the range of flora on display. Specialized areas include a shade garden, a butterfly garden, and a therapy garden.

Intergenerational Activities

On a typical day, a visitor to Kendal can see people ranging in age from three to 103—and every age in between. All of them consider Kendal to be their community, in part because of opportunities for members of all age groups to partner in various activities. This intergenerational approach has evolved into a formal program, in 2012 bringing national distinctions both to Kendal and to the city of Oberlin.

The presence of Kendal's Early Learning Center, located virtually

Resident Katherine Nunley with a young man from the Kendal Early Learning Center.

Resident Jean Eaton and two children from Kendal's Early Learning Center listened to instructions for the baking project they cooperated on as part of the intergenerational activities program.

in the center of the campus, is a major contributor to the intergenerational character of the community. Its 20-24 pre-kindergarteners regularly tour the entire campus, visiting residents in their homes and collecting stories, souvenirs, and their share of hugs and treats. Many residents also volunteer with the Early Learning Center, visiting with the children or helping out during their swimming sessions in the Kendal pool. The children also participate in baking, art, and music projects with residents in the Care Center every week.

Since the age range of seniors at Kendal spans more than four decades, they also develop intergenerational projects among themselves. An example is the One to One Baking project, in which younger residents who have trained to use the appliances in the "country kitchen" in Whittier help older residents in the Care Center who want to create favorite items using treasured recipes.

Jazz Listening Group

Befitting its subject, the Jazz Listening Group began as an improvisation. In fall 1995 a number of residents enrolled in a "Living Room Learning" course in American jazz offered at Kendal by Case Western Reserve University, hosted by the late resident Betty Spelman. The following spring, a few months after the course ended, residents began meeting on their own to continue the discussion and listening. Residents Ralph Turner and the late Hugh McCorkle were the conveners and handled the audio-visual equipment, and participants brought recordings from their own collections to share.

In recent years the leadership of the group has been taken up by Harvey Culbert and Del Jenkins, but its location remains the Whittier Lounge, which has excellent stereo equipment.

Jigsaw Puzzle Table

From the very earliest days of Kendal at Oberlin, a number of its residents have enjoyed jigsaw puzzles. Initially they worked at tables set up in the lounge areas in the apartment building, but in 1994 a puzzle table appeared in the Heiser Lounge.

At first only one person worked at the puzzles there, but soon others joined in. Residents from the Woodshop fabricated small trays so players could sort out puzzle pieces by colors and shapes, the latter with special names such as "spade foot/feet," "leaners," or "triples." The puzzle table in the lounge remains a point of interest for residents, visitors, grandchildren and their parents.

kaores.kendal.org (Residents' Web Site)

The World Wide Web made its debut in 1991, but access to it was still limited to highly specialized users when Kendal at Oberlin opened in October 1993. Over the following years it became clear that participation in the Web would be necessary for organiza-

Screen shot from the site on the World Wide Web maintained by the Kendal at Oberlin Resident's Association. Found at www.kaores.kendal.org.

tions whose activities depended on communications, and in 2009 KORA decided to develop a site to meet residents' needs.

A six-person committee chaired by Carl Peterson was appointed to work on the site, which went live at the end of 2009 with the URL of kaores.kendal.org, signifying that the site was initially hosted on The Kendal Corporation's web server. From its more simple origins, the site has grown to include links to menus, daily announcements, a complete listing of KORA committees and programs, links to community resources, updated weather forecasts, and news and feature articles with abundant illustrations. Resident Jim Pugsley, retired professor of electrical engineering from the University of Maryland, has served as webmaster since the beginning, and a KORA committee continues to oversee the web site, which is now hosted on an independent server.

Above: Members of the Kendal Trio at a 2010 performance included Wilma Weber (cello), Jane Hannauer (violin), and Cathryn Bacon (piano).

Opposite: Staff of The Kendalight *in its early years included residents Art Steele (left), editor, and Jane Buell. The publication has served as the community's principal news vehicle since 1993.*

Kendal Trio

In 2006, a local musician friend mentioned to resident violinist Jane Hannauer that Wilma Weber, a longtime music teacher from nearby Wellington, was moving to Kendal, and that she wanted to resume playing the cello in a chamber music trio. "Anybody interested?" she asked. Hannauer was, of course, and before long had also enlisted pianist and fellow resident Cathryn Bacon in the project, working initially on the Mendelssohn *Trio in D*. Later Jane Nord, another resident and an accomplished pianist, became involved with the group as well.

Over several years the trio has performed at a wide range of Kendal events, but the way that residents hear them perform most

frequently is during their open rehearsals in the Heiser lounge. One recently arrived resident walked by during a rehearsal and exclaimed: "What a classy place I've moved to! Live classical music in the morning!" Although they don't put it that way, children from Kendal's Early Learning Center must feel similarly when they attend Trio concerts or just hear their rehearsals.

The Kendalight

Perhaps no other local publication is read as widely or carefully as the monthly editions of *The Kendalight*, a newsletter that reports news and events from across the campus. The publication traces its origins to the "Ad Hoc Newsletter," an informal vehicle that began in 1993 as the community was first being settled, published initially by the Kendal administration. In November 1993 the late resident Art Steele became the editor and the name was changed to *The Kendalight*. Initially it ran only two or three pages in length, but grew gradually to its current standard size of 10 pages, with one issue hitting a dozen pages.

After eight years, Steele retired as editor and was succeeded by resident Betsy Thomas, who served until 2005. She was in turn succeeded by resident Elizabeth Aldrich, who continues as the current editor. Throughout the years a large group of Kendal residents have contributed writing and editing, a task made easier since 2008 when *The Kendalight* gained an email address so submissions could arrive electronically.

Paper copies of the newsletter are distributed to all residents' mailboxes by resident Don VanDyke, who also handles production of the copies, and they are mailed to priority list members and to other Kendal retirement communities. Issues also appear on the KORA web site.

Library

Even before Kendal at Oberlin opened in the fall of 1993, the residents-to-be formed a library committee. It was chaired by the late resident Bob Weinstock, who wrote to each committee member before the moving date to ask for ideas on policies and procedures. They decided that all materials for the library should be donated except for a paid subscription to *The New York Times*. In later years this policy has been relaxed, and some books and a number of periodical subscriptions are purchased.

The shelving and the initial boxes of donated materials arrived about simultaneously several weeks after the first residents moved into their units. The cataloging process was guided by the late resident Ben Custer, retired from the Library of Congress staff.

The library has aged well, and remains a vital component in the daily life of the campus. It was designed carefully, and its holdings and services are responsive to the changing needs of residents.

The marimba ensemble from the percussion department at the Oberlin Conservatory of Music has a tradition of performing annual winter holiday programs for residents and guests at Kendal.

Marimba Concerts

Almost every year since Kendal opened has seen a visit by a group of percussion students from the Oberlin Conservatory of Music for the annual Marimba Christmas Concert. Led by Professor Michael Rosen, director of the Division of Woodwinds, Brass and Percussion, the ensemble of a dozen or so students performs seasonal favorites for an audience of residents and their guests, often including young family members who have never seen live music played on instruments like marimbas, glockenspiels, xylophones, and vibraphones. The music is infectious, luring diners out of the Sunday brunch in the Fox and Fell Dining Room to seats set up in the Heiser Lounge.

Meet, Greet & Eat

Kendal at Oberlin imported this concept in 2011 after learning about its successful use at another Kendal retirement community. The goal is simple: to encourage residents to eat with people other than their regular dinner companions. Once a quarter, residents who have signed up for the program come to dinner, draw table numbers from a bin, collect their food from the buffet line, and join whoever else has drawn the same table numbers.

The program has been immensely successful, selling out its full complement of reservations each time it has been offered. Reports from participants are glowing, but the best indicator of how well the program works is reflected in the comments of one resident who participates regularly: "Listen to the noise level of the conversations," she notes. "They're with different people, so they haven't already heard what their table mates have to say!"

Memorial Program/Care and Nurturing Committee

After Kendal opened in 1993, religious institutions in Oberlin were called upon to organize memorial services for residents who died, many of whom were recent arrivals to the community. Soon it became clear that depending on local churches, temples, and other institutions to handle these events was unreasonable: in many cases residents had not formed local affiliations, and in others they did not identify with particular religious groups. Resident Paulie Evans played a leadership role in organizing a Kendal committee to plan and host memorial events, working with the families of deceased residents. This pattern continued with Nancy Garver as chair, succeeded more recently by Ardith Hayes.

The memorial program operates as a subgroup of the Care and Nurturing Committee of the residents association. Other programs under this banner include the Buddy System, which encourages residents to identify counterparts; Hospitalization, which tends to the needs and interests of hospitalized residents; Medical Companions, which arranges for residents to be accompanied to off-site medical appointments; SCC Shoppers, which organizes resident volunteers to shop weekly for other residents confined to the Stephens Care Center; Supporting Friends, which provides assistance to residents in the SCC; and the Wheelchair Brigade, a group of volunteers who transport wheelchair-bound residents to on-campus activities.

Miniature Golf Course

Located on the lawn just south of the Heiser Center's Fox & Fell Dining Room, the miniature golf course (sometimes called "Kendalopolis") traces its origins to the initiative of a particular Kendal resident. Ben Lenz wrote in an article prepared for Kendal's 15th anniversary in 2008:

Gnome at the fourth hole of the miniature golf course. (Photo courtesy Paul Schwaegerle)

> "Pam and I moved in with 60 pieces of 1½" x 1½" x 8' *pao lopi*, a tropical hardwood with a 60-year outdoor life guarantee. When I found that the putting green here at Kendal was not used a great deal, I asked the Sports Committee if I could build a miniature golf course on the putting green..."

Once assured that the project wouldn't damage the putting green—it rests lightly on the green's surface—the committee approved the project. Lenz recruited fellow resident Joe Luciano to help, and together they worked in the Kendal woodshop to build it. They designed obstacles and pathways, often having to redesign and rebuild them when they failed. One element of the course that unfailingly delights children who play the course is a xylophone whose tones ring out as the ball rolls along its path. That device needed the expert help of Oberlin College ethnomusicologist Rod Knight and the late physicist Roger Bacon.

Mt. Kendal

The construction of the classic cottages, the Heiser Center, and related buildings before Kendal first opened in 1993 involved con-

Above: The Kendal campus, as viewed from the portion of "Mt. Kendal" known as "Wildflower Hill." This area has been cleared of invasive plant species and is a favorite hiking path. (Photo courtesy Scott Orcutt)

Opposite page: Performance by the Oberlin Musical Union in Finney Chapel in December 2011. A significant number of singers in the ensemble — as well as many audience members — are Kendal residents.

siderable excavation. The excavated soil was moved to the north edge of the campus, where it was gradually shaped into a gentle ridge that serves as a border between the campus and a New Russia Township park. It is a modest rise that would meet no standard definition of a mountain, but it was dubbed "Mt. Kendal."

The ridge is self-planted with trees, shrubs, wildflowers, and thistles, has a path along the top of the ridge, and is a favorite hiking route for some. The western portion of the ridge has been tended by resident Betty Weinstock, rooting out thistles and other invasive species and planting a few wildflowers. For this reason the area is now known as "Wildflower Hill."

Music!

Many entries in this chapter refer to music as a favorite interest among Kendal residents. Some of those performances take place at Kendal at events coordinated by the Music Committee, chaired by Marian Lott and Allen Huszti.

Most performances occur at the Oberlin Conservatory of Music, however, and transportation can be an issue for residents who don't drive. The KORA Transportation Committee organizes bus service to take residents to and from musical events at the Conservatory and at related facilities. Phyllis Current chaired this program from the opening of Kendal in 1993 with the assistance of the late Paul Oncley, and was succeeded in 2008 by Allen Huszti. During his first year as chair, Huszti organized buses for 67 events during the academic year, more than half of which included two or three bus loads of attendees. In selecting the concerts to be covered, Huszti reports that instrumental and choral ensembles

The 1908 Carnegie Library Building at Oberlin College, built as a result of a gift from Andrew Carnegie, one of many donations he made to institutions and communities across the nation. It now houses classrooms and faculty and administrative offices.

seem to be most popular among residents, followed by faculty solo recitals and faculty ensembles.

Not all music is live, of course, and Huszti also leads a series of opera DVD concerts in the Kendal auditorium each year, drawing largely on his own extensive collection of recordings. An accomplished singer and instrumentalist and retired professor of music from Sweetbriar College, Huszti provides background information on each opera at these sessions.

Oberlin College and Conservatory

Founded in 1833, the same year as the city of Oberlin, the college is the main anchor institution and largest employer in the area. Kendal is located less than a mile away from the OC campus, an easy walk or bike ride for residents and students alike, and both groups have considerable experience making the trip to pursue a variety of opportunities:

Music. The curriculum at the Oberlin Conservatory of Music results in more than 400 concerts, recitals, operas, and other performances each year, most of them open to audiences, many at no charge. Ranging from classical to jazz, solos to large ensembles, and featuring performances by students, faculty, and visiting artists, these events take place mostly on the college campus, but some are scheduled at Kendal. For example, Kendalites of long standing recall fondly the visit by the St. Petersburg String Quartet when they were in residence at the Conservatory in the late 1990s and early 2000s.

Student mentoring. Each year Kendal residents serve as mentors for Oberlin College students enrolled in courses where regular contact with seniors is helpful. An example is a first-year seminar titled "*Ars Moriendi*: Death and the Art of Dying," in which students read and discuss literature, music, and art relating to death and dying. Students in the course meet with residents either at Kendal or at any of several locations in town.

Oberlin College students, alumni, and community residents gather at the annual "Illumination" event held on Tappan Square during commencement weekend. Primary lighting for the evening event is from lanterns.

Lectures and exhibits. Just as the year is filled with concerts and other performances, Kendal residents regularly attend lectures, art exhibits, and other presentations at the College and its Allen Memorial Art Museum. OC faculty and students are also frequent speakers at Kendal.

College courses. With the permission of the instructor, Kendal residents enroll at no cost as auditors (no grades or degree credit) in College courses that have space available. Some residents have also taught courses at the College, particularly in the Experimental College ("ExCo"), a program operated by students in which instructors can be faculty, students, or community members.

Play Readers

Play reading has existed at Kendal at Oberlin since January 1994, when the late resident Libby Steele led a group of twelve people in reading a play together one afternoon in the training room, a space that has since been converted to other uses. They continued on a monthly basis, eventually moving to the auditorium in the Heiser Center. In September 1994, the late Ruth Graf became the group's chair, and she donated scripts for 527 plays to the Play Readers' library.

Opportunities broadened in November 1998 when an improved sound and lighting system was installed in the auditorium. Warren Wickes, then chair of Play Readers, convened a meeting of residents in March 1999 to plan a program of evening performances in the auditorium for Kendal audiences. The first of these took place in January 2000. Since then more than 75 productions have been staged. In recent years, Play Readers chairs have included Katie Brown, Milt Garrett, the late Coby Swank, and Jerry Berner. Betty Weinstock developed a catalog of plays in the library in 2003, and it has been updated since then.

Since not all participants were equally interested in the staged readings, Jane Eddy established Play Readers II in November 1999 for those who wanted to stay with the original format of reading dramatic scripts with each other. In February 2006 Vi Blount revived this group, now called Drama Circle.

Precision Lawn Chair Drill Team

Kendal's Precision Lawn Chair Drill Team was started in 2004, inspired by Ben and Pam Lenz. Their daughter had called to tell them about a Patriot's Day parade in Rockport, Massachusetts, where she had seen such a routine performed. She urged her parents to start a similar group at Kendal.

The creator of the Rockport show, Duncan Ballantyne, shared

Kendal's Precision Lawn Chair Drill Team performing at the 2012 Independence Day program. Members, all of them Kendal residents, practice many times a year to achieve their trademark performance style, and are called on to participate in community and regional events as well.

his original routines with the Lenzes, some of which continue to be performed to this day. Others were rejected, however: "Walking backward or spinning chairs overhead would overload both our Care Center and the local osteopaths," Ben Lenz explained.

The group performs to great acclaim at events such as Oberlin's annual Big Parade in May, where it is regularly one of the main features of the town parade, at Kendal's celebration of Independence Day on July 4, and at other community events that request its participation. Composed entirely of Kendal residents, the team executes carefully but zanily choreographed routines involving garish costumes, attempted (and often successful) march steps, and self-effacing humor, all done while toting folding lawn chairs. Fun is had by all.

Publicity Plugs

The Oberlin City School District is small, with limited administrative staffing. For example, there is no staff member charged with providing information to news media. In a meeting with school leaders in 2004, Kendal at Oberlin CEO Barbara Thomas proposed a program to be called "Publicity Plugs" that would engage Kendal residents with experience as writers and reporters to prepare stories about the schools for local newspapers.

The response was enthusiastic, and eight residents signed up – two for each school building in the district. The founding Publicity Plugs reporters were Claudine Carlton, Alan Carroll, the late Eva Greenberg, Thelma Morris, Ruth Searles, Martha Stacy, Etta Ruth Weigl, and the late Jim White. In the ensuing years others have stepped forward to succeed some original members of the group. Coordination has been provided since the beginning by Nancy Freed of Kendal's marketing staff.

The value of Publicity Plugs was recognized almost immediately, and has been confirmed many times since. In 2006 the Association of Philanthropic Housing and Services for the Aged (AOPHA) conferred its Public Trust Award on Kendal in recognition of the program, and AOPHA's Ohio chapter presented its Social Commitment Award the same year. In 2009 the *Oberlin News Tribune* chose Publicity Plugs as "Oberlinians of the Year," an honor usually awarded to an individual. Later in 2009 the American Association of Housing and Services for the Aging gave the program its Public Trust Award. In 2012 the Ohio School Boards Association named the program to its Media Honor Roll.

Quaker Values and Practices

Although the Kendal system is independent of any religious institution, the organization was founded and is led with "a strong regard for the principles of the Religious Society of Friends (Quakers)."[24] Those values address virtually every aspect of living and working at Kendal, as these few examples selected from a much longer list will illustrate:

- "To enhance the quality of life and vitality of those we serve and to foster a sense of community…
- "To encourage and welcome all people…
- "To engage in practices that sustain and improve our environments…
- To foster a high quality work experience for staff…"[25]

Each of these values is also put into practice with specific actions that serve to shape the culture at each Kendal site. At Kendal at Oberlin, these values also are addressed periodically in presentations by administrators and by residents who bring considerable experience with Quaker life. The long tenure among Kendal staff members also suggests that this approach benefits employees as well—it is mirrored in the human resource policies for the organization.

RAF Shop

New residents have almost always arrived at Kendal with more furniture and other belongings than they need. At the same time, there has always been a commitment at Kendal to make it possible for residents whose resources do not last as long as their lives to continue to stay in the community. These two situations fit together.

The Residents Assistance Fund, which makes it possible for residents to remain in the community after their own funds are exhausted, is supported in part through the sale of items not needed by other residents. The first RAF sale took place in summer 1994, less than a year after the first residents arrived, and was chaired by the late Evelyn Young. The follow-

Above: Nancy Garver modeling an outfit at the 2013 style show sponsored by the RAF Shop, which supports the Residents Assistance Fund. Residents and staff members modeled clothing and accessories from the RAF Shop.

Opposite page: Basket of holiday ornaments on display at the RAF Shop's annual holiday sale.

ing summer, new residents Nancy and Len Garver were tapped to serve as co-chairs, which they agreed to do "without knowing what we were getting ourselves into." Ernie Eddy helped, as he had the previous year, and a mountain of items was hauled over to First Church on Oberlin's Tappan Square for the sale, which brought out a huge crowd from the city. The sale also thinned out the closets and pantries at Kendal.

After the 1995 sale, resident Ruth Schwaegerle suggested that

Above: The 1994 rummage sale, the first organized to sell excess items brought by arriving Kendal residents, was held in First Church in Oberlin. Ernie Eddy, who helped coordinate the sale, is shown in the background.

Opposite page: Margaret-Ann Ellis addressing the "haggis," a Scottish delicacy, at the 2013 Robert Burns birthday celebration, with visiting piper Glen Wright. Chef Scott Stonestreet (right) prepared the haggis.

the annual sales be converted into an ongoing shop on the Kendal campus. Since 1996 the RAF Shop has operated out of two locations in the apartment building, supplemented by occasional sales in cottages or apartment units being vacated. Leadership for the RAF Shop rotates among residents, with Ruth Ann Clark serving as chair at this writing. Sales of used cars—an important source of revenue for the Residents Assistance Fund—were handled from the beginning by Ernie Eddy, who was succeeded in 2008 by Sam Goldberg.

Robert Burns Dinner

Beginning in 1999, Kendal residents have gathered each January to celebrate the anniversary of the birth of the poet Robert

Burns. Initially it was Scots and their spouses who participated in the event, many wearing "tartans, sporrans, or scarves." In more recent years all residents with any heritage in the British Isles, or even those who would like to hail from that part of the world, have been invited.

Regular portions of the program include a parade through the facility led by a uniformed bagpiper, a formal haggis ceremony, and stories and proclamations offered by hosts as well as guests at the dinner in the dining room. Kendal chef Scott Stonestreet has developed a reputation for the way he prepares haggis, the traditional Scottish delicacy.

Science Discussion Group

About a year after Kendal opened in 1993, resident Ralph Turner was having lunch with the late Tom Protzman. Their conversation turned to science, a topic in which they were both interested. They continued meeting weekly for lunch and extended their conversations on science, never coming close to exhausting the subject or their own interest. Finally they wondered whether others might like to join the discussions as well, so they publicized the idea and found many takers—not surprising, since many Kendal residents have backgrounds in the sciences.

The Science Discussion Group now meets monthly, not to exchange rarified and advanced knowledge among experts in one or more of the sciences, but rather to discuss issues and trends in the sciences "broadly defined," as the founders of the program intended. Non-experts are welcome to participate, and the discussions are lively and informative.

Silliness Committee

This group's members, always anonymous, are responsible for unpredictable cartoon blitzes and the occasional "flamboyance" of flamingos (that's a collective noun for a group of the pink birds) to celebrate important events.

Observant residents will sometimes note a lone flamingo stationed outside a cottage or apartment in the early morning hours with a sheaf of papers attached to its neck. The papers are "adoption" documents with the following message:

> "Congratulations! The Silliness Committee welcomes you to membership… There are no meetings, no chair nor any president. The rules are few and hereby set forth:
>
> - "To try to be kind to fellow residents who may be developmentally disabled in the humor department.
> - "Do not throw toilet paper rolls over the trees, strew marbles on the

Thanks to the Silliness Committee, flamingos and other visitors appear in unusual spots.

floor or grease the sidewalks.
- "Seize opportunities to make people laugh…
- "Emulate the Flamingo Brigade by sometimes striking at odd hours.
- "Remember that it is easier to get forgiveness than permission.
- "No explosives."

Many residents—as well as the local constabulary—undoubtedly appreciate that final rule.

SPINACH

In 2004, residents May Zitani and the late Leslie Farquhar were talking in the Heiser Lounge. Their conversation turned to food, and they found they shared an interest in nutrition and its effects on health. Nancy Hultquist joined them and the "Healthy Eaters Group" was formed, with regular dinner gatherings of residents with similar interests. Later Pam Lenz suggested the acronym SPINACH ("Senior People Interested in Nutrition and Community Health"), and the new name was adopted.

At the group's first dinner meeting, on August 25, 2004, Ben Lenz provided fresh peaches and melon and May Zitani brought low-fat desserts. The after-dinner discussion, led by Don Hultquist, concluded that the group would meet monthly, that all interested residents would be invited, and that the agendas for the meetings would feature informal discussions about new nutritional information, tips for healthy eating, and possibly recipes. The pattern continues, with regular sessions convened over dinner in the William Penn Room.

Spring Fling

The name may be self-explanatory and perhaps a bit trite, though the event itself arrives each April as a fresh reminder that the

Fitness Center staff member Saun Howard (center) led a tap-dance trio that also featured residents Nancy Hultquist (left) and Eileen Dettman at the 2013 Spring Fling event in the well-decorated auditorium.

bleak months of winter do indeed vanish. It's a social evening, with music, games, and refreshments, amid seasonal decorations in the Heiser Center auditorium. In recent years the decorations have grown more and more remarkable thanks to resident multimedia artist Ted Nowick and his band of crafters.

Staff-Resident Potluck

Kendal's calendar of events during the winter holidays is daunting to say the least, with more than a dozen seasonal programs offering nourishment for the mind, the heart, the soul, and the body. Many take place in the evenings, after most staff members have departed for the day. The annual staff-resident potluck, however, is deliberately scheduled over the lunch hour so that all can attend. As the name suggests, everyone brings some food to the party in the Fox and Fell Dining Room, where staff and residents are encouraged to mingle at tables.

Student Staff in Dining Services

As noted elsewhere in this history, Kendal's residents deeply appreciate the organization's staff. Most of them are regular, full-time employees, some of whom have worked on the campus for many years. That staff is supplemented by part-time student employees, most of whom work as servers and wait staff in Dining Services, where their high school schedules can be accommodated with some ease. Ann Pilisy, director of the dining rooms, has recruited and trained these students since Kendal opened in 1993. In the early years their numbers were much smaller, but more recently, she reports, Kendal has consistently received "tons of applications" for the positions. In many cases, the student employees acquire their first real work experience at Kendal.

Student staff in Dining Services planning to graduate from high school in June 2013 gathered in the Cafe outside the Fox & Fell Dining Room to celebrate with residents. Ann Pilisy, who directs the dining rooms and trains and supervises the student workers, is second from left.

Resident Jerry Berner tried his hand against a table tennis "robot" server during the 2012 Fun Fitness Week events.

The largest numbers of Kendal's student employees tend to come from Oberlin High School, Firelands High School, and the Lorain County Joint Vocational School. Several other area schools are regularly represented as well, however. High school affiliations usually become more obvious at two points of the year: when student workers (in formal attire) bring their prom dates to Kendal to meet residents and staff colleagues, and at the annual graduation party for students completing high school. Pilisy also often organizes an annual "alumni reunion" of sorts for former student employees in the spring, calendars permitting.

In addition to the high school students, Pilisy has hired a smaller number of students from Oberlin College and Lorain County Community College.

Table Tennis

From the start, thanks to the gift of a table from the late resident Mary Miraldi, table tennis has formed part of Kendal's recreational scene. In the early years, activity focused chiefly on a yearly tournament, while efforts to spur regular play surfaced periodically and then faded. Beginning in 2007, led by resident Sidney Rosenfeld, a growing number of residents began improving their games, and the term "table tennis" gained currency in the Kendal community, pushing aside the more common term "ping-pong." The core group expanded to some 14 enthusiasts, and play moved from a hallway into Kendal's auditorium, using an upgraded table, soon to be augmented by a second table thanks to generous gifts from residents. More recently a third table, a top-of-the-line JOOLA model, has also been added.

As this is written, the group plays three times weekly with ITTF-approved inverted rubber paddles, dozens of good practice balls, full-surround barriers, and three ball scoops to spare tired backs. Top Ohio player Keith Pech occasionally visits to help group members hone their skills in small-group sessions.

Ranging in age from their 70s to early 90s, the group of enthusiasts keeps growing, using table tennis to focus their minds, brighten their spirits, invigorate their bodies, and widen their social circles.

Tennis Courts

The vision that inspired the small group that led the development of the tennis courts at Kendal was both practical and far-sighted: they were eager to have a clay surface on the courts "so that older adults would find play easier on their knees, hips, and ankles." Residents Ken Roose, Betty Weinstock, and the late Bill Renfrow visited other sites under construction to see the techniques being used. This same trio provided financial support for the pro-

Tennis courts under construction in early 1994. The courts employ a clay surface to minimize damage to the joints of players.

ject. Ultimately the clay surface was applied by Lee Tennis Courts Products, an affiliate of Lucky Stone Corp., in Charlottesville, VA, a nationally known source of clay court coatings.

The courts opened in June 1994, less than a year after the community's first residents arrived, when 25 Kendal residents assembled on the courts to nail down the last of the tapes that marked the boundaries of play. The surface and the hardware used for the courts continue to this day to meet the needs of Kendal's players.

Third Thursday Lecture Series

As Kendal is a community filled with people who love to hear about and discuss ideas, it should come as no surprise that the Third Thursday Lecture Series has been a fixture since 1994. Speakers have been drawn from Oberlin College, from the region, and from among Kendal's own residents.

The lectures may be on virtually any subject so long as they represent important issues, although the planners try to avoid topics that are likely to be addressed by other groups, such as health, nutrition, information technology, history/heritage, science, genealogy, or the environment. Speakers must limit their remarks to 45 minutes or less, followed by questions and open, active discussion. The series is organized by residents; its current chair is Priscilla Steinberg. In keeping with the community's flexible approach to many issues, "Third Thursday" events can take place on other days of the month when appropriate.

Trains and Trolleys

Although Oberlin currently has no rail transportation options, the Kendal community is well stocked with trains and trolleys because of the interests of its residents.

When residents Don and Joyce Parker moved to Kendal in 2009, they arranged to bring along a large portion of the "Hoot

Above: Resident Len Garver (far right) and Rod Knight, professor emeritus of musicology from Oberlin College and Conservatory, demonstrate the trolley system Garver began building decades ago, replicating an actual trolley system in Milwaukee, Wisconsin, from that era.

Opposite page: Resident Don Parker operating the "Hoot 'n' Holler" Railroad, a large G-gauge layout that he and his wife brought with them to Kendal. Parker operates the train on a regular schedule.

'n' Holler Garden Railroad" they had developed at their home in Cinnamon Lake, Ohio. Don had been involved in designing and building garden railroads for many years, and is a contributing writer for *Garden Railways Magazine*. The installation at Kendal includes more than 300 feet of G gauge track, seven bridges, three trestles, and a tunnel, with two complete trains. Parker drove a golden spike into the layout at the unveiling in September 2009 before an appreciative audience of residents and their children and grandchildren. Demonstrations occur regularly.

Long-time resident Len Garver has a smaller model layout, though it dates back much further – to his early interest in trolleys as a teen, when he began developing a working scale model of a portion of a 1950s-era trolley system in Milwaukee, Wisconsin. He constructed every element himself except for the model trolley cars. The system runs off overhead electric wires similar to those actually used by urban trolleys, and—just as in real life—the two trolley trains follow an intricate pattern of intersecting routes, requiring careful control by the operators to avoid collisions. Garver and his friend and collaborator, Oberlin College professor emeritus of ethnomusicology Roderic Knight, schedule viewings of the trolley layout regularly.

Other rail aficionados in Kendal's history include the late Bill Hayward and more recent arrivals John Pesuit and Dan Reiber.

Transportation

Some Kendal residents do not have their own vehicles anymore, and even those with cars often prefer to take advantage of one or another of the transportation options available to residents.

Donna Smith, Kendal's transportation coordinator, arranges rides to medical appointments and to local retail outlets using Kendal vehicles. At this writing, responsibility for arranging transportation to special events is divided among a trio of Kendal residents: Allen Huszti, who arranges rides to musical events; Pat Talbot, who sets up "big bus" trips to museums and other destinations, and Priscilla Steinberg, who arranges transportation for all other events. In addition, a group of residents volunteer to provide transportation on a one-on-one basis for other residents who need to get to health care appointments outside the standard coverage.

Drawing on this rich mix of options, Kendal residents are able to get where they need to go even when they no longer use their own vehicles.

The Troll Bridge

One of the most direct pedestrian routes from the Heiser Community Center to the northeast quadrant of the Kendal campus runs across a small wooden bridge over an even smaller stream. When resident founders Alan and Nancy Gage arrived in 1993, they soon

Residents performing in the 1995 Winter Solstice program, which adopted a Mayan theme. From left: Nick Stevenson as the corn god, Alice Shaver as the sun god, and Art Steele as the chief god.

noticed that the sound of people crossing the bridge reminded them of a classic children's story, "The Three Billy Goats Gruff." Nancy, a multi-talented artist, crafted doll-sized trolls that Alan built into a protected display that sits on the bridge railing.

Winter Solstice

From the very beginning of Kendal at Oberlin, residents have mounted musical productions that carry on the ancient ritual of marking the shortest day of the year, when the noonday sun appears at its lowest point above the horizon and the season of winter formally begins.

The community's first official winter solstice program took place on December 21, 1995, Kendal's third winter holiday season, drawing on traditions associated with ancient and modern

Above: The Solstice Chorale, directed by Helen Taylor, performing at the 2012 Winter Solstice program. The backdrop for the stage, a view of the night sky showing an "analemma," was created by resident Bob Cothran.

Opposite page: The late Duncan Love at work in the woodshop.

Europe, African American culture, and music and reading from several religions, as well as a national organization known as "Revels" that dates back to the early 1970s in Cambridge, Massachusetts. The focus of subsequent performances has varied over the years, from replicas of English performances and nostalgic looks at the music of the 1930s through the 1960s to multicultural collages of music and stories from many different parts of the world—all with costumes and often with dance. These performances inevitably draw overflow audiences to the auditorium to see residents perform. The event is traditionally followed by a reception in the Heiser Lounge.

Woodshop

At the very beginning of Kendal at Oberlin a large room was designated for a woodshop in an area of the Heiser Center that also included horticulture and crafts spaces. Over the years, the wood-

shop has received gifts of hand and power tools from incoming residents. At this writing it contains a table saw, miter saw, two band saws, drill press, planer/joiner, lathe, router, belt sander, drills, along with a large number of hand tools, a substantial supply of various screws, nails, hooks, paints, varnishes, and stains, and four large workbenches.

In 1996-1997, the woodshop expanded into the adjacent horticulture space to establish a "clean area" where handwork can be done without the threat of sawdust from power tools. A complicated but efficient exhaust system was designed and installed largely by resident Alan Gage, who with fellow resident Ernie Eddy have been key players in the woodshop. Jim Helm is the current chair of the woodshop committee.

Use of the woodshop requires only a one-time nominal fee, which gives residents access to the full range of tools on hand. While many members work on personal projects, they also take on repair and construction projects for other residents, for the Kendal community, and for the Oberlin area. The value of the woodshop to residents is highlighted in the experience of the late Sam Moore, an experienced and skilled craftsman who regarded his woodworking activities as so important to his wellbeing that he negotiated special access to a workbench in the shop as part of his contractual arrangement with Kendal at Oberlin when he applied for admission. He spent many rewarding hours at his workbench during his years at Kendal.

Residents Al and Polly Carroll tried out the "country kitchen" area that was built into the expanded facilities of the Whittier Assisted Living Wing.

Chapter VII

Forward!

> *"Would you tell me, please, which way I ought to go from here?"*
> *"That depends a good deal on where you want to get to," said the Cat.*
> *"I don't much care where—" said Alice.*
> *"Then it doesn't matter which way you go," said the Cat.*
>
> Exchange between Alice and the Cat in
> Lewis Carroll's *Alice in Wonderland*

About a decade ago, Beloit College in Wisconsin began a custom that has gained a large following not only in higher education but in the broader society as well. Drawing on their understanding of the cultural experiences of each year's entering freshmen, a member of the Beloit faculty and the school's public affairs director assemble an annual "mindset list," a set of characteristics that may distinguish those students from their predecessors, and ultimately from their successors as well.

Much of the history of Kendal at Oberlin has reflected the experiences of its prospective and current residents, or at least what the organization believes those experiences have conditioned these residents to prefer in a retirement community. At any one time, the existing residential community is composed of individuals whose ages may be forty years or more apart, placing them in quite different experiential cohorts. Underlying all of that, of course, is the set of continuing values and principles associated with Kendal, with the city of Oberlin, and with Oberlin College and Conservatory that make this a genuinely unique community.

Resident Joe Luciano (second from right) conducts "Joe's Class," regular water aerobics sessions for members of the Oberlin community to promote health. He was a practicing physician in Oberlin for many years, including several years after he and his wife Dorothy moved to Kendal.

How can we expect the experiences and characteristics of future residents of Kendal at Oberlin to affect the way our successors will live here?

As this history has looked back at 20 years of life here at Kendal, let's look ahead now 20 more years, to a couple arriving in 2033. They will be 68-year-old post-Baby Boomers, born in 1965. They're coming to Oberlin from a large city in the northeast. Based on what we know today about their lives and what we can project about the next two decades (and with apologies to Beloit College), their profiles might look something like the following:

- At age 68, they have opted for early retirement ("normal" retirement age has been raised to 70).
- Both have worked—or sought work—for their entire adult lives, but this has involved employment in two to four different careers for each of them.
- They lost their home in the "great recession" of 2008-

09 and felt the lingering effects of that downturn for another decade. They have lived in a condominium for 15 years.
- Their employment patterns have caused them to live in five different states and one foreign country.
- They have never known a time when Medicare and Medicaid did not exist, or when there were no controversies about their continued existence.
- Social Security exists and will provide them with a modest stipend, but they are overwhelmingly dependent on their own retirement savings for most of their living expenses.
- Apple II computers were donated to their schools when they were in the fourth grade, and they have been using computers ever since.
- They both had email addresses before they graduated from college in 1987, and cell phones five years later.
- While electing to live in a retirement community, both plan to continue their professional activities, ideally as consultants.
- Their children and grandchildren live on both coasts and in Asia, so a large fraction of their visiting is done electronically.
- They have worshiped in a nondenominational religious center near their former home and are seeking a similar affiliation in Oberlin.
- They are vegetarians, and they plan to garden.
- They expect to live at Kendal for at least 30 more years.
- He is Latino, she is African American.

Developing detailed specifications for a Kendal environment

Don Reeves (left), president of the Kendal at Oberlin Residents Association, and Creative Arts Therapy Director Michele Tarsitano-Amato (center) received the 2013 Community Partner of the Year award from Bo Arbogast of Oberlin College's Bonner Center for Service and Learning. Kendal was honored for providing opportunities for OC students to work as interns and volunteers, and for a history of collaboration.

that would meet the needs and expectations of a couple such as this in 2033 is beyond our current capabilities, and would not belong in a history of Kendal in any case. But the policies and principles that have been described in this history are characteristics of a community that can adapt to the preferences of prospective residents like these, even as they also help those residents understand the value of traditions and customs associated with a living, learning, and caring community reaching that will by that time be its 40th year of existence. Resident engagement in governance and decision making; careful financial and program planning; emphasis on intergenerational activities; continuing close ties to the town and to Oberlin College and Conservatory; and a strong commitment to continuing care are among the features that promise to be as valuable for the future as they have been in the past two decades.

Features that seem likely to play even stronger roles than in the past include leadership in renewable energy and a reduced carbon footprint, avenues for continuing residents' professional development and service, and improved integration into the health care systems of the region, consistent with emerging trends in the nation's approach to this crucial topic. Issues of affordability and diversity will also be key topics of discussion for the future.

To ensure that the activism and engagement that have characterized the last two decades continue into the future, Kendal can count on the energy and imagination of its current residents and the mechanisms they have created. These range from resident-driven activities, in cooperation with a strong, devoted staff, and such vehicles as the Residents Archives Committee, which serves as a repository of information about residents and their activities, to the continued presence of lively, talented high school and college students as part-time staff and volunteers, and to periodic gatherings to renew our familiarity with basic Kendal values and Quaker principles.

It is worth returning to the late Tom Piraino's reference to the era of stagecoach transportation in the American west in describing an ideal future for Kendal:

> "Let us hope for, and work for, having everyone in our community be first-rate, third-class ticket holders on the Kendal at Oberlin stagecoach."

The talented hands of resident and master weaver Mary Louise VanDyke at work at her loom in the Hobby Room.

Appendices

Founders

Given the effort of the planners of Kendal at Oberlin and the pioneering spirit of its early residents, the community gives special attention to those who moved in during the first three months of operation—October, November, and December 1993. They are known as the "Founders." Below are their names, shown in the order of their arrival in each of those three months. Asterisks indicate those who were deceased as of July 2013.

October 1993
*Custer, Benjamin A.
 Custer, Emiko H.
*Funkhouser, Mary L.
*Moore, Samuel A.
*Moore, Jane H.
*Reynolds, Harriet
*Wright, Elizabeth L.
*Bassett, Virginia Ruth
*Boase, Marjorie B.
*Boase, Paul H.
*Boase, Constance W. Flanigan
*Holbrook, Dorothy B.
 Hutchison, Janet B.
*Hutchison, William M.
 Long, Charlotte R.
 Long, Herbert S.
*Tibbetts, Katherine K.
*Tibbetts, William D.
*Balogh, Sara C.

 Hunt, Esther C.
*Largent, Robert M.
*Largent, Vera M.
*Regli, Constance W.
*Svete, Irene E.
*Young, Keith R.
 Young, Victoria K.
*Coffin, Frances D.
*Coffin, Kenneth P.
 Morgan, Maxwell G.
 Morgan, Muriel P.
*Verlie, E. Joseph
*Verlie, Elizabeth E.
*Young, Evelyn
*Jones, Eddythe M.
*Merritt, Helen K.
*Schwimmer, Helen M.
*Sprow, Clementine H.
*Stephens, James T.
*Stephens, Jeanne H.

*Stevenson, Nicholas
*Baum, Marian H.
*Foreman, Marion B.
*Peterson, Lois G.
*Renfrow, Antoinette S.
*Renfrow, William B.
Adams, Margaret Ellen
Evans, David
Evans, Mary C. ("Paulie")
*Jones, Owen T.
*LeBeau, Constance J.
*LeBeau, Marjorie M.
"Milliken, Elizabeth
*Miraldi, Mary K.
*Schaeffer, K. H.
Schaeffer, Eunice B.
Schwaegerle, Edward G.
Schwaegerle, Ruth C.
*Hoerr, Janet U.
*Singleton, Robert C.
*Singleton, Wanda R.
*Spelman, Gordon
*Spelman, Kathleen M.
*Taylor, Richard W.
*Taylor, Sadie W.
*Brashares, Charles M.
*Brashares, Edith O.
*Byles, Janet K.
*Byles, G. Huntington
Current, Phyllis
*McCorkle, Hugh F.
McCorkle, Lois P.

*White, James W.
*Baker, Ruth S.
Gage, Alan
Gage, Nancy
*Laird, Helen E.
*Laird, John H.
Lester, Catharina D.
Weigl, Etta Ruth
Eddy, Ernest
Eddy, Jane
*Kurtz, Edith M.
*Canalos, G. Virginia
*Cotabish, Alice M.
Daffin, Norma
*Flynt, Mary A.
*Lewis, Mary Jane
*Histed, Margaret E.
Richards, Louise S.
*Simonson, Roy W.
*Simonson, Susan M.
*Stocker, Beth K.
Ailey, Mary F.
*Ailey, Robert J.
*Spelman, Elizabeth L.
*Worcester, Florene E.
*Slajnar, Millie
*Smith, Audra C.
Weinstock, Elizabeth B.
*Weinstock, Robert
*Ernst, Joan K.
*Milliken, Elizabeth D.
*Christie, Bettie L. (moved away)
*Heath, Elaine

November 1993
*Gabalac, Frieda
*Hasse, Frances S.
*Hasse, Gordon W.
*Kane, Ellen
*Neill, Elizabeth M.
*Stiles, Elizabeth W.
*Wilcox, Dorothy H.
*Fisk, Mary W.
*Lucioli, Clara E.
*Prescott, Polly
*Prescott, Katherine
*Meints, Nelle G.
*Sable, Doris S.
*Lilie, Ellen Anna
*MacKay, Gladys G.
*MacKay, James A.
*Stechow, Ursula
*Johnson, Jr., William C.
*Warch, Pauline R.
*Warch, Willard F.
*Steele, Arthur R.
*Steele, Elizabeth
*Appleton, Linda S.
*Appleton, Lloyd O.
*Gladieux, Bernard L.
*Champney, Kathlyn B.
*Metcalf, Sarah H.
*Mosher, Harriet J.
*Geissal, Marjorie N.
*Dixon, Elizabeth M.
*Wagner, Helen
*Rotermund, F. Elisabeth
*Simpson, Alice H.

*Thompson, Priscilla E.
*Smith, Miriam Waldron
 Wright, Jean F.
*Neavill, Elizabeth B.
*Poporad, Anna
*Arthur, Margaret R.

December 1993
*Burton, Anne H.
*Cook, Margaret J.
 Dugan, Joyce S.
*Hallock, Jeffrey
 Hallock, Myriam L. (moved away)
*Hallock, Richard R.
*Hanson, Ruth E.
*Metzger, G. Herbert
*Metzger, Madelyn L.
 Roose, Gretchen
 Roose, Kenneth
*Arnold, Paul B.
*Arnold, Sarah C.
*Buck, Jane
*Licklider, Adelaide
*Licklider, Templin
*Leonard, Barbara
*Leonard, Margaret
*Melcher, Anna S.
*Reichard, Joe
*Reichard, Anita
*Anderson, David
 Anderson, Molly
*Farnsworth, Charles
 Farnsworth, Kathryn

*Runyan, Elizabeth
*Runyan, William
*Shaver, Alice
*McIlroy, Amy
*McIlroy, Donald
*Mitro, Eleanor
*Lapham, Lowell
*Dexter, Lewis (moved away)

Turner, Ralph
*Walker, Mary Emma
*Walker, William
*Yinger, Milton
*Yinger, Winnie
VanDyke, Don P.
VanDyke, Mary Louise

Aerial view of the Kendal at Oberlin campus, looking toward the northwest. Shown at the bottom left are the Phase I cottages. Cottages in Phases II and III, now located in the area near the top edge of the image, were not yet started when this photograph was taken.

Current Kendal at Oberlin Residents

The list below represents all residents living at Kendal at Oberlin as of July 2013, and includes their former residences and the years in which they came to Kendal.

Adams, Margaret Ellen .... Wellesley, MA, 1993
Ailey, Mary Frances ("Frampie") .... Ashtabula, OH, 1993
Albright, Marilyn ("Lyn") .... Lancaster, PA, 2005
Aldrich, Elizabeth .... Chagrin Falls, OH, 2004
Anderson, Madeleine ("Molly") .... Oberlin, OH, 1993
Andrews, George and Marlene .... Oberlin, OH, 2009
Ashbrook, Mary .... Berea, OH, 2001
Augustine, Mary .... Labadie, MO, 1996

Bacon, Agnes K. .... Strongsville, OH, 2002
Bacon, Cathryn .... Amherst, OH, 2008
Baldwin, Helen and Robert .... Nashville, TN, 2005
Barna, Barbara .... Berea, OH, 2011
Barnett, Naomi .... Oberlin, OH, 1996
Baughman, Barbara .... Sandusky, OH, 2005
Baznik, Donna and Richard .... Cleveland Heights, OH, 2010
Beauchamp, Nancy .... Troy, MI, 2000
Bent, George and Ruth Schoeni .... Rocky River, OH, 2006
Berner, Jeanne and Jerome .... Shaker Heights, OH, 2002
Bimber, Constance and Russell .... Painesville, OH, 2000
Blodgett, Jane .... Oberlin, OH, 2008
Blount, Viola .... Hendersonville, NC, 2005
Bolland, Janet and Thomas W. .... Athens, OH, 2004
Boren, Wynona .... Washington, DC, 2001
Breese, Louise .... Rocky River, OH, 2006
Brinkman, Elizabeth .... Springfield, OH, 2000
Brown, Catharine ("Katie") .... Tampa, FL, 1998
Bruer, Barbara .... Hartsdale, NY, 2011
Burkhard, Barbara Daschbach and Richard .... Westlake, OH, 2007

Busiel, Joanne ....Asheville, NC, 2011

Carlson, Florence ("Bobbie") ....Oberlin, OH, 1995
Carlton, Claudine and Terry...................................Oberlin, OH, 2001
Carrell, Demaris ("Demmie") ....Oberlin, OH, 1995
Carroll, Alan and Polly..Shoreham, NY, 2003
Carson, Marilyn (and Barry Walker)................ Floral Park, NY, 2012
Chisholm, Corning...Bratenahl, OH, 2002
Clark, David and Ricarda ("Ricky")......................Oberlin, OH, 2006
Clark, Ruth Ann (and Ardith Hayes).................... Oak Park, IL, 2011
Coan, Cynthia and Robert.................................. Milltown, NJ, 1998
Collins, Charlotte................................. Melbourne Beach, FL, 2000
Cook, Dennis and Judy .... Laurel, MD, 2013
Cooke, Vera...White Plains, NY, 1998
Cooper, Nancy ....Oberlin, OH, 1998
Cooper, Frances ("Fran") and Roger....................Oberlin, OH, 2005
Cothran, Robert.. Knoxville, TN, 2009
Culbert, Harvey (and Louise Luckenbill)...........La Grange, IL, 2002
Current, Phyllis... Bradley Beach, NJ, 1993
Custer, Emiko.. Bethesda, MD, 1993

Daffin, Norma.. Berea, OH, 1993
David, Betsy and Martin ("Tin")........................ Middleton, WI 2013
Davidoff, Martin .... Catonsville, MD, 2011
Davis, Anne ....Shaker Heights, OH, 2012
Deist, Marcia .... Akron, OH, 2011
Dettman, Eileen...Boone, NC, 1996
Devereux, Eleanor ....Asheville, NC, 2007
DeWitt, Betty .... Ithaca, NY 1997
Didchenko, Rostislav ("Rosti") .... Middleburg Heights, OH, 2009
Donner, Mae Alice .... Maple Heights, OH, 2003
Dugan, Joyce .... Perry, OH, 1993
Dunn, Arlene and Larry ....LaCrosse, IN, 2013

Eaton, Jean ....Vinalhaven, ME, 1994
Eckstein, Bernard and Sheila.......................No. Royalton, OH, 2002

Eddy, Ernest and Jane .... Hudson, OH, 1993
Elder, Anne Cartmell and John .... University Park, MD, 2007
Ellenberger, Janette .... Brecksville, OH, 1998
Ellis, Margaret-Ann and Milton .... Massillon, OH, 2004
Erdy, Virgina .... Lorain, OH, 2009
Evans, David and Mary C. ("Paulie") .... Oberlin, OH, 1993
Evans, Marie .... Oklahoma City, OK, 2009

Farnsworth, Kathryn .... Englewood, NJ, 1993
Farquhar, William .... Oberlin, OH, 1999
Fauver, Catherine .... Walnut Creek, CA, 2012
Ferguson, Janet .... Kalamazoo, MI, 2001
Fischer, Gay .... Cupertino, CA, 2009
Fletcher, Michael .... Mechanicsburg, PA, 2011
Fordyce, Beverly and Stuart .... Fairview Park, OH, 2008
Freas, Pauline .... Oberlin, OH, 2006
Friedman, Edward and Lois C. .... Houston, TX, 2007
Frierson, Andrew .... New York, NY 2013

Gage, Alan and Nancy .... Racine, WI, 1993
Gallagher, Eugene and Marilyn .... Lexington, KY, 2003
Ganzel, Carol .... Oberlin, OH, 2006
Garrett, Jane and Milton .... Cleveland, OH, 2000
Garver, Leonard and Nancy Bradford .... Schenectady, NY, 1994
Gold, Margaret (and Len Singer) ..... Hastings-on-Hudson, NY, 1995
Goldberg, Marcia and Samuel .... Oberlin, OH, 2004
Gordon, John and Peggy .... Hudson, OH, 2011
Graham, Jean Susan .... Adrian, MI, 2001
Greenberg, Nathan .... Oberlin, OH, 2005
Grove, Mary Lynne .... So. Euclid, OH, 2006

Haessly, Rita .... Ruskin, FL, 2008
Hamilton, Jim .... Rocky River, OH, 2006
Handman, Pauline (and Paul Spierling) .... Katonah, NY, 2011
Hannauer, George and Jane S. .... Cranbury, NJ, 2002
Hatton, Howard .... Oberlin, OH, 2002

Hayes, Ardith (and Ruth Ann Clark).................... Oak Park, IL, 2011
Hayward, Shirley .... Forest City, CA, 1996
Hefner, Leslie and Robert .... Ann Arbor, MI, 2011
Heller, Jean... Elyria, OH, 1996
Helm, Annemarie ("Anne") and James .... Oberlin, OH, 2010
Helper, Eleanor.. Columbus, OH, 2003
Henke, Herbert and Sabra C. .... Oberlin, OH, 2001
Hoffmann, Randi .... Ann Arbor, MI, 2012
Hofman, Feite ("Fred")... Oberlin, OH, 2001
Hultquist, Donald and Nancy S. .... Ann Arbor, MI, 2002
Hunt, Esther.. Lorain, OH, 1993
Huszti, Allen... Madison Heights, VA, 2007
Hutchison, Janet .... Cleveland Heights, OH, 1993

Ijiri, Tomoko and Yuji .... Pittsburgh, PA, 2012
Illig, Donald and Joylynn ....Simsbury, CT, 2001
Ingersoll, Fern and Jay............................... Takoma Park, MD, 2005

James, Elizabeth .... Cleveland Heights, OH, 1995
Jenkins, Adelbert ("Del") and Betty .... New York, NY, 2006

Kahn, Diana and Ron..Oberlin, OH, 2013
Kanost, Margaret.. Lake Orion, MI, 2013
Kay, Marvin ("Mike")..Toledo, OH, 1996
Kellner, Eileen...Hartsdale, NY, 2010
Ketcham, Helen .... Litchfield, OH, 1997
Koerner, Gerlind .... Beverly Hills, MI, 1998
Kohl, Alice ....Rocky River, OH, 1999
Koster, Mary Jane.. Brecksville, OH, 1996
Krato, Darlene .... St. Claire Shores, MI, 2000

Lamb, Harold .... Silver Lake, OH, 1995
Langeler, George .... Oberlin, OH, 2006
Laurell, Gaye (and Daniel Reiber)...................... Mayfield, OH, 2011
LeGrand, Raymond .... The Villages, FL, 2011
Lenz, Benjamin and Pamela .... Sea Cliff, NY, 2002

Lester, Catharina ("Katy") .... Akron, OH, 1993
Lewis, Arn and Beth .... Wooster, OH, 2011
Lewis, Irwin ("Irv") .... Strongsville, OH, 2006
Lindamood, Jane .... Columbus, OH, 1999
Long, Charlotte and Herbert .... Cleveland, OH, 1993
Long, Russell ("Rusty") .... Cape Canaveral, FL, 1999
Long, Edward .... North Wales, PA, 2010
Longsworth, Carol and Robert .... Oberlin, OH, 2011
Lott, Marian J. .... Akron, OH, 2006
Love, Nina .... Annandale, VA, 2004
Luciano, Dorothy and Joseph .... Oberlin, OH, 1994
Luckenbill, Louise (and Harvey Culbert) .... Falmouth, MA, 2009

Marshall, Elizabeth .... Oberlin, OH, 2012
Marshall, Jim and Linda .... Huron, OH, 2013
Martin, Anne (and Tom) .... Fayetteville, NY, 2010
Martin, Tom (and Anne) .... Oberlin, OH, 2012
Maurushat, Jocelyn .... Sandusky, OH, 2009
McCalla, Mary Beth .... Sidney, OH, 2001
McClusky, Nancy and Robert .... Bethesda, MD, 2009
McCorkle, Lois .... Cleveland Heights, OH, 1993
McQueen, Albert .... Oberlin, OH, 1995
Michalak, Bernice .... Marathon, FL, 1995
Mihu, Jean .... Vermilion, OH, 2004
Miller, Ruth .... Richmond, VA, 2006
Moore, Jane Ross .... Brooklyn, NY, 2005
Moreland, Jean .... Fairview Park, OH, 2012
Morgan, Maxwell and Muriel .... Cleveland, OH, 1993
Morris, Thelma J. .... Shaker Heights, OH, 2005
Murphy, Jerry .... Orwell, OH, 2003
Myerly, Joyce and Richard .... Hendersonville, NC, 2009
Myerson, Marilyn .... Washington, DC, 2007

Nord, Jane .... Oberlin, OH, 2006
Norenberg, Don and Joanne .... Fairview Park, OH, 2006

Nowick, Theodore (and Robert Taylor) .... Blue Hill, ME, 2003
Nunley, Katherine .... Shaker Heights, OH, 2000

O'Connor, Elizabeth .... Elyria, OH, 2009
Olmsted, Clarence ("Bush") and Levona .... Cleveland, OH, 2005
O'Neil, June .... Sheffield Village, OH, 1997
Orcutt, Adrienne ("Adie") and Scott .... Medina, OH, 2009

Palmieri, Joseph and Susan .... Oberlin, OH, 2009
Paré, Diantha and Victor .... Oak Ridge, TN, 2009
Parker, Don and Joyce .... West Salem, OH, 2008
Parrott, Anne .... Davis, CA, 2006
Payton, Eileen and John .... Beachwood, OH, 2003
Perhamus, Ernest .... Huron, OH, 2004
Pesuit, Harol and John .... Briarcliff, NY, 2011
Peterson, Carl .... Oberlin, OH, 2005
Porter, Larry and Marjorie .... East Lansing, MI, 2013
Potter, Ann .... Wheeling, WV, 2001
Pugsley, Emily and James .... Silver Springs, MD, 2009

Randel, Helen and Robert .... Huron, OH, 2008
Reed, Melissa .... Piqua, OH, 2012
Reeves, Barbara and Don .... Central City, NE, 2009
Reiber, Daniel (and Gaye Laurell) .... Mayfield, OH, 2011
Reid, Margaret ("Peggy") .... Fairview Park, OH, 2007
Rice, Mary Jean and William .... So. Euclid, OH, 1997
Richards, Louise .... Cleveland Heights, OH, 1993
Rider, Margaret ("Kay") .... Green Valley, AZ, 2013
Roose, Gretchen and Kenneth .... Boynton Beach, FL, 1993
Rosenfeld, Sidney and Stella .... Oberlin, OH, 2007
Rutherford, Isobel .... Cleveland, OH, 2009

Schaal, David and Jean S. .... Iowa City, IA, 1998
Schaeffer, Eunice .... Cambridge, MA, 1993
Schneider, Alverta .... Albuquerque, NM, 2008
Schoonmaker, Dina and Richard .... Oberlin, OH, 2009

Schreiner, Kathryn and William..........................Hinckley, OH, 2000
Schultz, Margaret ("Peg") ....Pittsboro, NC, 2007
Schuster, Melvin ....Oberlin, OH, 2012
Schwaegerle, Catherine ("Cate") and Paul ....Oberlin, OH, 2007
Schwaegerle, Edward and Ruth C. ....Elyria, OH, 1993
Schwartz, Howard ....Shaker Heights, OH, 2003
Searles, Ruth ....Toledo, OH, 2002
Shaw, Julia .... Hudson, OH, 2000
Shearer, John and Mary Ann........................... Stillwater, OK, 1997
Shoemaker, Louise..Queensbury, NY, 2011
Simons, Mary..Washington, DC, 2004
Singer, Leonard (and Margaret Gold) .... Berea, OH, 1998
Sook, Lois ....New York, NY, 2002
Spierling, Paul ("Bud") (and Pauline Handman) Katonah, NY, 2011
Stacy, Martha..Oberlin, OH, 2002
Steinberg, Ira and Priscilla...................................Oberlin, OH, 2009
Stunkel, Eva ....Sarasota. FL, 2013
Sunshine, James .... Tiverton, RI, 2005
Swartwout, June .... Morgantown, WV, 2002

Talbot, Patricia ....Homewood, IL, 2007
Tandy, Judith.. Patagonia, AZ, 2011
Taylor, Helen.. Newton, MA, 2009
Taylor, Robert (and Theodore Nowick) .... Blue Hill, ME, 2003
Thomas, Elizabeth...Grafton, OH, 1996
Thompson, Catherine ("Cay") .... St. Louis, MO, 2003
Tompos, Grace.. Wooster, OH, 2012
Trump, Richard... Santa Fe, NM, 2001
Turner, Ralph ....Oberlin, OH, 1993

VanDale, Carla and Robert .... New Wilmington, PA, 2013
VanDyke, Don and Mary Louise ....Oberlin, OH, 1993
VanRaaphorst, Donna........................Broadview Heights, OH, 2008

Walker, Barry (and Marilyn Carson) ....Rockville, MD, 2006
Walworth, Frank and Joy ....Cleveland Heights, OH, 2005

Wanyek, Janet .... Wakeman, OH, 2011
Wardwell, Anne and Edward .... Shaker Heights, OH, 2006
Weber, Wilma .... Wellington, OH, 2006
Weigl, Etta Ruth .... Webster, NY, 1993
Weinberg, Herbert .... Ashland, OR, 1998
Weinstock, Elizabeth .... Oberlin, OH, 1993
Werner, Janet Kelsey and R. Budd .... Athens, OH, 2007
Wheeler, Margaret .... Berea, OH, 1995
Whitehead, Eleanor .... Elyria, OH, 2008
Wickes, Warren .... Hudson, OH, 1998
Wilber, Catherine .... Oberlin, OH, 2011
Wilcox, Anne and George .... Mentor, OH, 2004
Wright, Jean .... Oberlin, OH, 1993

Young, Victoria ("Torie") .... Beverly, NJ, 1993

Zeitlin, Aideen and Gerald .... Chestnut Hill, MA, 2013
Zinn, Grover and Mary .... Oberlin, OH, 2011
Zitani, May .... Cedar Grove, NJ, 2003

Kendal at Oberlin Residents Association

Even before Kendal's first residents arrived in fall 1993, plans were made to create an association to represent them in the new community. Known as the Kendal at Oberlin Residents Association (KORA), the group serves the interest of residents in a wide range of areas, from planning and other issues involving Kendal's administration to organizing and strengthening resident activities and services. KORA's Council, elected resident representatives, meets monthly in open session, and its committees meet more or less frequently as needed.

Presidents of the Kendal at Oberlin Residents Association

Joseph Verlie, 1994-95
Jane Eddy, 1996-97
Ruth Schaeffer, 1998-99
Joseph Luciano, 2000-01
Thomas Piraino, 2002
Leonard Singer, 2003
Alan Gage, 2004
Mary Ashbrook, 2005-06
Thomas Piraino, 2007
Robert Taylor, 2008
Nancy Hultquist, 2009-10
John Elder, 2011-12
Donald Reeves, 2013-

Staff with Ten or More Years of Service

Staff members play key roles at Kendal, and those with long tenure inevitably come to be regarded as "family members" by residents. Among retirement communities, Kendal is also fortunate that an unusually large share of its staff members have remained with the organization for many years, a feature that is often cited by residents as an important element in defining the overall character of the campus.

The following continuing staff members, listed here by the year in which they first came to Kendal, have been employed at the organization for at least ten years.

1992 (Founding Staff)
Nancy Freed, Admissions & Marketing
Barbara Thomas, Chief Executive Officer

1993 (Founding Staff)
Rebecca Bolyard, Facility Services
Rebecca Butler, Human Resources
Laurie Dupee, Senior Independence (originally Health & Wellness Clinic)
Jon Hall, Facility Services
Dorothy Holzhauer, Stephens Care Center
Theresa Lanham, Kendal at Home (originally Health & Wellness Clinic)
Judith Miller, Accounting & Information Service
Anna Pilisy, Dining Services
Michele Tarsitano-Amato, Creative Arts Therapy
Ramie Ybarra, Dining Services
Beverly Zimmerman, Stephens Care Center

1994
Sarah Allen, Stephens Care Center
Laura Auble, Stephens Care Center
Jill Connone, Fitness Center
Joseph Dembek, Facility Services
Julie Price, Kendal's Early Learning Center
Margaret Stark, Admissions & Marketing
Bonnie White, Dining Services

1995
Lisa Blackford, Dining Services
Sandra Bockmore, Stephens Care Center
Janice Foster, Stephens Care Center
Katherine Helke, Stephens Care Center
Theresa Kovach, Admissions & Marketing
Elizabeth Martinez, Stephens Care Center
Jean Nickles, Stephens Care Center
Regina Shumate, Stephens Care Center

1996
Patricia Johnson, Stephens Care Center

1997
Virginia Wolf, Administration

1998
Linda Beveridge, Stephens Care Center
Kimberly Blair, Finance
Majoretta Brantford, Stephens Care Center
Jennifer Comerford, Stephens Care Center
Ruth Jasko, Stephens Care Center
Susan Kuncel, Stephens Care Center
Toni Merleno, Human Resources

1999
Laura Diedrick, Dining Services
Jeffrey Emerick, Dining Services
Monica Fuquay. Dining Services
Blair Loudermelt, Dining Services
David Patterson, Facility Services

2000
Darlene Brown, Stephens Care Center
Patricia Hill-Holcomb, Senior Independence (originally Health & Wellness Clinic)
JoDee Palmer, Admissions & Marketing
Kim Preston, Social Services
Jennifer Rimbert, Facility Services
Suzanne Rogers, Stephens Care Center
Kimberly Rollin, Stephens Care Center
Phyllis Saxon, Stephens Care Center

2001
Ann O'Malley, Finance
Gregory Wilgor, Facility
    Services

2002
Robyn Becher, Stephens Care
    Center
Debora Gail, Stephens Care
    Center
Susanne Rollins,
    Administration
Stephanie Sutton, Dining
    Services
Tori Webster, Dining Services

2003
Lynne Giacobbe, Kendal at
    Home
Crystal Hall, Housekeeping
Kay Herrick, Stephens Care
    Center
Robin Jones, Kendal's Early
    Learning Center
Deborah Lindner,
    Housekeeping
Ryan Stalzkowski, Facility
    Services
Lisa Stewart, Stephens Care
    Center
Bonnie Valentine-Byrd, Facility
    Services
Jane Webster, Finance

Board of Directors

The Board of Directors (previously the Board of Trustees) is the principal governance organization for Kendal at Oberlin, which is an independent, nonprofit corporation. The directors are responsible for the long-term health of the community, including selecting and evaluating its management, safeguarding its physical and financial assets, approving policies and strategies for the institution, and securing resources to support its operation and growth. The Board of Directors is a self-perpetuating body of interested people, and includes several Kendal residents among its members. Directors receive no compensation for their service.

Chairs of the Kendal at Oberlin Board of Directors

Stephens, James, 1987-90
Carrell, Jeptha, 1991
Piraino, Thomas, 1992-94
Bent, George, 1995-2001
Dunn, Richard, 2002-03
Picken, John, 2004-07
Tolbert, Melva, 2008-10
Sabath, Nancy, 2010
Picken, John, 2011-12
Clark, Jon, 2013 (interim)
Ed Miller, 2013-

Members of the Board of Directors

Anderson, Susan, 2008
Andrews, George, 2006-13
Bent, George, 1992-2003
Bojanowski, Carol, 2008-13
Brittingham, Midge, 2012-13
Browne, Errol, 2008-2013
Burgess, Liz, 2012-13
Carrell, Jeptha, 1987-95
Clark, David, 1987-94
Clark, Jon, 2010-13
Clash, David, 2010-13
Cook, Dan, 2011-13
DeBouter, Vance, 2011-13
Distelhorst, Garis, 1997
Dunn, Richard, 1995-2004
Dye, Nancy *(ex officio)*, 1995-2005
Edgerton, John, 1997-2002
Elder, John, 1987-91
France, Evelyn, 2000-03
Gardner, Daniel, 2004-08
Haber, Mary, 2012-13
Heiser, Karl, 1987-91
Helm, Anne, 2002-10

Hewitt, David, 1995-99
Hoffmann, Michael, 2005
Holliman, James, 2005-07
Hutchison, Janet, 1991-95
Jensen, Ann, 1987-99
Keating, Susan, 2006-07
Keeney, Elizabeth, 1997-98
Kinley, John, 1995-2000
Koeblitz, William, 1987-96
Krislov, Marvin *(ex officio)*, 2010-13
Lancaster, Sydney, 1999-2003
Lewis, Erin, 2005-06
Livingston, Dayton, 1995-2003
Long, James, 1987
Luciano, Dorothy, 1987-98
Luciano, Joseph, 2002-04
Martz, Pradnya, 2004-07
Mason, Emma, 2008-11
McKee, Mary, 2012-13
Meese, William, 2009-10
Melecki, Richard, 1999-2002
Miller, Ed, 2010-13
Nizza, Jane, 2005-07
Norton, Jane, 2001-08
O'Toole, Dennis, 1999-2007
Picken, John, 2001-13
Piraino, Thomas, 1990-95
Protzman, Ferdinand, 2008-13
Ramp, Marjorie, 1995-2003
Reichard, Anita, 1987-94
Rice, William, 2005-13
Ricker, Alison, 2012-13
Rivers, Therese, 2006-07

Roose, Diana, 2001-09
Sabath, Nancy, 2006-10
Schwaegerle, Edward, 1987-92
Shaeffer, Ruth, 2002-09
Shields-Kyle, Eldonna, 2006-12
Singleton, Robert, 1994-98
Springfield, Freddie, 1999
Stephens, James, 1987-92
Stilwell, David, 2001-08
Taylor, Sadie, 1996-2001
Taylor, Robert, 2009-13
Thomas, Robert, 1987-89
Thomas, Betsy, 1999-2004
Tolbert, Melva, 2005-10
Treuhaft, Paul, 1997-2004
Waite, Jan, 1990, 1992-97
Wiles, Stephanie, 2010-11
Yood, Nancy, 1996-98
Young, Keith, 1999-2001

Glossary of Kendal Names

Even a casual visitor to Kendal at Oberlin is bound to wonder about the namesakes and other origins of names in use for various areas of the community's campus. Below is a short glossary of nomenclature in common use. The author is indebted to the anonymous author of an earlier version of such a glossary that included some of these terms.

Den: A small private dining area located in the Fox & Fell Dining Room in Heiser Center. The room can be totally closed off from the main dining area.

Fox and Fell Dining Room: The largest of Kendal's three dining areas is named for the late George Fox, founder of the Religious Society of Friends (the Quakers), and his wife Margaret Fell, a noted social reformer.

Hallie's Alley: Walkway through the woods in the eastern part of the Kendal campus, named for the late resident Hallie Laird (see chapter 6, "Our Favorite Things").

Heiser Community Center: Karl and Ruth Heiser were among the founders of Kendal at Oberlin, though neither ever moved in because they both died before their dream was realized. Karl's mother grew up in a noted Quaker family (the Harveys) in Clinton County, Ohio. The Heiser Center contains common dining, lounge, and meeting facilities, the library, the auditorium, activities spaces, and staff offices.

Jameson Wing: The skilled nursing care wing C of the Stephens Care Center is named for George C. Jameson, who was a physician in Oberlin from 1893 until his death in 1948. He was a leading proponent of community health and sanitation measures, and a crusader for medical ethics at a time when medical quackery was rampant.

Kendal: The name of the community—and of the national organization that has launched affiliate communities in several states—comes from that of an English town in the northern Lake District. Located in the "dale" or valley of the river Kent, the town was called "Kendale," ultimately shortened to "Kendal." George Fox, the founder of Quakerism, spoke to followers in Kendal many times, and years later his wife Margaret Fell used the name for the fund she raised to meet living expenses that exceeded the means of their followers.

"Kendalight" vs. "Kendalite:" In many ways this is a traditional community, filled with people who want to use nomenclature correctly. Let it be noted that *The Kendalight* is the monthly newsletter for residents that has been published since the community opened in 1993, while a "Kendalite" is a resident of Kendal at Oberlin. For a while there was some disagreement about this, but it seems to have been resolved within the community's first decade.

Kendalopolis: The tongue-in-cheek name given to the putting green just outside the Fox & Fell Dining Room. The space now houses a miniature golf course.

Langston: The informal dining room in Heiser Center is named for the late John Mercer Langston, one of Oberlin College's most distinguished African American graduates. An abolitionist, attorney, and diplomat, he was the first dean of the law school at Howard University.

Mount Kendal: Again, a tongue-in-cheek name for the gentle rise along the northern boundary of the Kendal campus created by soil from the excavation work done for the original buildings. It's not a mountain by any standard, but it's the highest point on the campus. The western two-thirds of the rise is known as "Wildflower Hill," where residents have eliminated invasive species in favor of native plants.

Neighborhoods: The Kendal campus consists of several residential areas, many of which celebrate their special characteristics and identities. Some have adopted names, such as "The Upper East Side" (cottages near lots 5-7); "The Lower East Side" (cottages near lots 8-10); "The Outback" (cottages near lots 1-4); and "The Meadowlands" (Phase I). Other areas have names as well, though they seem less well entrenched.

Patterson Wing: The skilled nursing care wing B in the Stephens Care Center is named for 1862 Oberlin College graduate Mary Jane Patterson, the first African American woman to earn a bachelor's degree. She went on to a career as a teacher, and was the principal of a black high school in Washington DC.

Penn: A large dining area in the Fox & Fell Dining Room that can be closed off to accommodate groups. It is named for William Penn, the Quaker leader and philosopher who founded the Pennsylvania Colony.

Phase [I, II, or III]: Three clusters of 12 cottages each that were built between 2006 and 2011 to accommodate additional residents. At this writing, efforts are under way to assign more traditional Kendal names to the clusters. For new residents and visitors the names present a dilemma, since most assume that "Phase I" should refer to the first cottages (i.e., "classic cottages") to be built on the campus.

RAF Shop: The thrift shop operated by residents to benefit the Residents Assistance Fund, which helps those who are unable to continue to support themselves financially after living at Kendal for a number of years. Despite occasional references to the Sopwith Camel and cries of "keep 'em flying," the shop is not a far-flung outpost of England's Royal Air Force.

Stephens Care Center: The care center at Kendal at Oberlin is named for the late Drs. James and Jeanne Stephens, founding residents of the community. They were among the founders of the Oberlin Clinic, and were deeply engaged in a variety of other community activities. Jim Stephens served for a period of time as chair of the early planning group that worked toward creation of Kendal of Oberlin.

Troll Bridge: The foot bridge joining the apartment building's parking lot with the complex of cottages in the northeast quadrant of the Kendal campus. A handrail on the bridge features a case displaying a set of small "trolls," an allusion to the fairy tale of the "Three Billy Goats Gruff." Residents Alan and Nancy Gage have been the chief proponents of the "troll" theme.

Whittier Wing: The assisted living wing in the Stephens Care Center is named for John Greenleaf Whittier, the noted 19th century abolitionist and poet. He used his influence to generate support for Oberlin College.

Persons Interviewed for this History

The author's connection with Kendal at Oberlin began only in 2010, when he and his wife moved to the community. To gather a longer view of Kendal's development and growth, interviews with the following individuals took place starting early in 2012. Not listed here are more informal discussions with residents and observers of the community that have also been very helpful but have not been as carefully recorded or documented. The author extends his gratitude to each of these interviewees.

- Paul Arnold (now deceased), former resident and professor emeritus of art at Oberlin College and a widely acclaimed artist in several media.

- Connie Boase (now deceased), a Kendal Founder and an active member of the community.

- Demmie Carrell, resident and widow of Jeptha Carrell, former executive director of the Nordson Foundation and an early member of the planning group for Kendal and chair of the institution's board of trustees.

- David Clark, resident and former vice president of Oberlin College; member of the planning group that worked on creating Kendal at Oberlin.

- John Elder, resident and former president of the Kendal at Oberlin Residents Association; former pastor of First Church in Oberlin, United Church of Christ.

- Shirley Hayward, resident and widow of Bill Hayward, whose lively communication activities helped others get to know Kendal in the 1990s.

- Don and Nancy Hultquist, residents of Kendal since 2000. Nancy served as president of KORA in 2009 and 2010.

- Dorothy Luciano, scientist, writer, resident, and early member of the planning group whose work led to the creation of Kendal.
- Ann Pilisy, director of dining rooms at Kendal at Oberlin since September 1993.
- Thomas Piraino (now deceased), former resident and member of the planning group; first chair of the board of trustees for Kendal; former president of the Kendal at Oberlin Residents Association.
- Maggie Stark, director of admissions and marketing for Kendal of Oberlin since May 1994.
- Michele Tarsitano-Amato, director of creative arts therapy, who joined the staff in August 1993
- Barbara Thomas, chief executive officer of Kendal at Oberlin since 1992.
- Ralph Turner, resident and professor emeritus of psychology at Oberlin College.
- Don VanDyke, Kendal Founder, retired Oberlin physician, and long-time administrative volunteer.
- Kathe Yerkes, director of dining services, The Kendal Corporation.

Advisory Committee for the History of Kendal at Oberlin

A writer taking on a venture of this scale needs wise, well-informed, and continuing advice from others whose perspectives are different and whose experience is often much longer. In this project the author has been assisted and guided in important ways by a small advisory committee of residents whose suggestions and other contributions are deeply appreciated. Members of the committee include:

- Connie Boase
- Martin Davidoff
- John Elder, *ex officio*
- Thelma Morris
- Dina Schoonmaker
- Priscilla Steinberg
- Don VanDyke

Note that Connie Boase was an active participant in the work of the advisory committee until her death in 2013.

The late resident Helen Schwimmer reading to children in Kendal's Early Learning Center. Interactions such as these are valuable and frequent.

Notes to the Text

[1] From Barbara E. Parsons, *An Act of Faith: The Kendal at Longwood Story* (Kennett Square, Pennsylvania: The Kendal Corporation, 1988, reprinted in 1993).

[2] From remarks to a meeting of new Kendal residents by Thomas Piraino, resident and former member of the Kendal at Oberlin board of trustees and former president of the Kendal at Oberlin Residents Association. Found on the web at kao.kendal.org in July 2010.

[3] Anita Reichard was one of the founding members of the planning group that nurtured the development of Kendal at Oberlin, and she and her husband, Joseph Reichard, were among its founding residents. The two Reichards preserved a large file of documents from the planning process, which were made available after her death in 2010.

[4] Oberlin College Archives, "RG 30/64 George E. Simpson (1904-1998)," accessed 3/4/2012. For this material and related information, see oberlin.edu/archive/holdings/finding/RG30/SG64/biography.html.

[5] Charles Durrett and Kathryn McCamant, quoted in Charles L. Belk, "Cohousing Communities: A Sustainable Approach to Housing Development," produced in conjunction with the University of California at Davis Extension Service, fall 2006.

[6] Karl F. Heiser, letter dated "March, 1987," and addressed to "Dear fellow Oberlinian."

[7] Comment by Marcia Heckert, a long-time member of Kendal of Oberlin's administrative staff, in the July 2003 issue of "Ripples in the Pond," a newsletter for Kendal's staff employees.

[8] Jeptha Carrell, "History of Kendal at Oberlin," July 1991. Carrell wrote this unpublished narrative of the early planning and development steps taken to create Kendal at Oberlin, drawing on his experience as a member of the original planning group and later as a member and chair of the Community Board.

[9] David Hewitt, quoted in Jeptha Carrell, op. cit.

[10] *New Russia Township Land Use Plan*, November 2001, ch. 1, p. 1. Found on the web at newrussiatownship-oh.gov/cms/images/documents/zoning_land_use_plan2001.pdf.

¹¹ Resident Benjamin Custer, speaking at the ribbon-cutting ceremony on October 6, 1993, for Kendal at Oberlin, as reported in the December 1993 issue of *News from Kendal at Oberlin*, p. 2.

¹² Esther C. Hunt, in a hand-written reminiscence on the occasion of the tenth anniversary of Kendal at Oberlin, October 2003.

¹³ Dorothy Holbrook, in a reminiscence on the occasion of the tenth anniversary of Kendal at Oberlin, October 2003.

¹⁴ Letter to residents and priority members from Tom Piraino, chair of the Kendal at Oberlin Community Board, dated November 24, 1994.

¹⁵ Dorsky Hodgson + Partners, Kendal at Oberlin Post-Occupancy Review, April 1998.

¹⁶ Richard J. Dunn, letter to residents of Kendal at Oberlin, issued in 2002 (undated). Cited in memo from Dave Schaal, resident and member of KORA Council, concerning "Growth Evaluation Process," dated July 22, 2002.

¹⁷ Schaal, *op. cit.*

¹⁸ Richard J. Dunn, letter to Kendal at Oberlin residents dated December 2, 2002.

¹⁹ Kendal at Oberlin Master Planning Committee, Report of Charrette No. 1, July 30, 2003.

²⁰ Center on Budget and Policy Priorities, "Chart Book: The Legacy of the Great Recession," updated December 11, 2012. On the web at www.cbpp.org/cms/index.cfm?fa=view&id=3252.

²¹ Kendal at Oberlin, Disclosure Statement, May 2007, p. 1.

²² *Ibid.*

²³ Stacy Terrell, "Kendal at Oberlin Quarterly Health Services Forum," January 2013.

²⁴ The Kendal Corporation, *Values and Practices*, 2012 edition, p. 23. This booklet is a summary of Kendal's guiding principles that has been updated regularly since 1987.

²⁵ *Ibid.*, pp. 3-4.

Index of Topics

AARP Tax Advisors, 86
actuarial analysis, 29-30
"Ad Hoc Newsletter," *see Kendalight*
Admiral at the Lake, 32
Advisory Committee, vi, 183
aerial views, 12, 161
Affordable Care Act, 96
Allen Memorial Art Museum, *see* Oberlin College
Allen Memorial Hospital, *see* Mercy Allen Hospital
anniversary, fifteenth, 99
anniversary, fifth, 63
AOPHA, 133
architect selection process, 30
architecture, 30; classic cottages, 74, 75; design elements, 31-32, 62-63; Dorsky, William A. and Associates, 30-31; Phase cottages, 75-78, 88, 90, 91, 92, 179
art, 100-102
Ashland College, 24
assisted living, *see* residential units
Audio Announcements, 102-103

Big Bus trips, *see* transportation
Big Rock Pond, *see* Rock Pond
Board of Directors, *see* directors
bofoellesskabe, *see* co-housing
Bonner Center, see Oberlin College
Buddy System, *see* Care and Nurturing Committee
butterfly garden, *see* horticulture
Buttonbush Bridge, 93
Buttonbush Pond, 67

Canoe, *see* Fleet
Cardinal Shop, 103
Care and Nurturing Committee, 51; Buddy System, 124; Hospitalization Committee, 124; Care and Concern Committee, 124; Medical Companions, 124; Memorial Program, 124-125; SCC Shoppers, 124; Supporting Friends, 124; Wheelchair Brigade, 124
Carter Nursing Home, 33
Cartmel community, 74
Case Western Reserve University, 118

CCRC, *see* continuing care retirement community
Center Pond, 65, 108
Ceramics Group, 103-104
Certificate of Need, State of Ohio, *see* nursing care facilities
Channel 19, 68-70, 104
characteristics, resident population, 60-61
Chicago, Kendal facility, *see* Admiral at the Lake
child care, 77
co-housing, 3-4, 39
coat hangers, 41
committees, resident, 51
Community Art Walls, *see* art
community building, 32
community gardens, 105
CommUnity Picnic, 67
CON, *see* Certificate of Need
Coniston community, 74
construction, Kendal at Oberlin, 34, 35, 41; Kendal at Oberlin, topping off, 38
Continuing Care Retirement Community, philosophy, x
cottage numbering system, 43-44
country kitchen, 152
Courtyard Garden, 85, 95, 105

Crosslands, Kendal at, 7, 31, 36, 74

Dartmouth College, 8, 14, 96
dining, healthy, 71
dining areas, Den, 177; Fox & Fell, 77, 123, 141, 177; Langston, 77, 178; William Penn Room, 179
Dining Services, student staff in, 141-143
Directors, Board of, 175-176
Dorsky Hodgson Parrish Yue, *see* architecture
Dorsky, William A. and Associates, *see* architecture
Drama Circle, *see* Play Readers

Economic impact, 82-83
economic trends, 86-88, 92-94, 154-155
energy conservation, 50, 75
environmental practices, 75
Eureka!, 106
evaluation, post-occupancy, 59-63
"ExCo" courses, *see* Oberlin College
Exercise Group, 107
expansion, 65, 71-78

Farmer's Pond, 65

188   HISTORY OF KENDAL AT OBERLIN

Fertilizer Fund, *see* financing

financing, project, 19-21, 28, 33, ; Bank of Ireland, 29; budget, 29

Firelands High School, 143

First Church in Oberlin, 9, 10, 35, 38, 135-136

Fitness Committee, 110

flamingos, *see* Silliness Committee

Fleet, the, 108

Food Committee, 51, 70

Founders quilt, 48-49

Founders, 46, 47, 48, 159-162

Fox & Fell, *see* dining

Friends Gallery, *see* art

Friends, Religious Society of, 7; Quaker values and practices, 133-134, 157

Fun Fitness Week, 110-111, 142

Geese, 111-112

Genealogy Interest Group, 112-113

governance, Kendal at Oberlin Community Board, 30; Kendal at Oberlin, 91-92

government relations, 32-34

Grandparent Readers, 80-81

Granville, Kendal at, 32,

Green Pond, 65

groundbreaking, 22-25, 27, 35

Hallie's Alley, 113-114, 177

Hanover, Kendal at, 8, 10

Hazard Reporting Committee, 53

Health and Wellness Clinic, Kendal at Oberlin, 97

Health and Wellness Newsletter, 114-115

health care, 3, 94-97; Slow Medicine, 96-97

Heiser Community Center, 38, 45, 48, 77, 123, 140, 150, 177

Heiser Pond, *see* Center Pond

Helping Hands committee, 53

Hidden Pond, *see* Woodland Pond

hobby room, 158

home health care, *see* Senior Independence

Hoot 'n' Holler Railroad, *see* trains and trolleys

horticulture, 115-116; Horticulture Committee, 84, 105, 116

Hospitality Committee, 67

Hospitalization Committee, *see* Care and Nurturing Committee

House Committee, 52

Hudson, Kendal on, 114

Illumination, *see* Oberlin College

Independence Day, 62, 109
independent living, *see* residential units
intergenerational activities, 116-117
interviewees, list of, vii, 181-182
Island Pond, 65

Jameson skilled nursing area, *see* Stephens Care Center
Jazz Listening Group, 118
jigsaw puzzles, 118
Judson Retirement Community, 36
JVS, *see* Lorain County

Kaores.kendal.org, *see* web site, residents'
Kendal at Home, 78, 90
Kendal Collects, *see* art
Kendal Communities, 8, 29
Kendal Continuing Care at Home, *see* Kendal at Home
Kendal Corporation, The, 23-24, 25, 28, 29, 31, 32, 34, 36,
Kendal Creates, *see* art
Kendal Gallery, *see* art
Kendal Management Services, 11, 15, 21,
Kendal Northern Ohio, 90

Kendal, origin of name, 177-178
Kendal's Early Learning Center, 77, 86, 110, 116, 117
Kendalight, 67, 85, 121-122
Kendalopolis, *see* miniature golf
KMS, *see* Kendal Management Services
KORA, *see* Residents Association

Landscaping, 64
Langston, *see* dining
laundry facilities, 59
Lawn Chair Drill Team, Precision, 131-132
LCCC, *see* Lorain County
Lexington, Kendal at, 115
Library of Congress, 122
Library, Kendal, 122
Longwood, Kendal at, ix, 23, 31, 36, 74
Lorain County, 15, 33, 82; Lorain County Community College, 143; Lorain County Joint Vocational School, 143

Management Assistance for Nonprofit Agencies (MANA), 82
marimba concerts, 123

Meadow Pond, 67, 113

Medicaid, 3, 155

Medical Companions, *see* Care and Concern Committee

Medicare, 3, 44, 155

Meet, Greet & Eat, 123-124

Memorial Program, *see* Care and Nurturing Committee

Mercy Allen Hospital, 21

Milwaukee, WI, *see* trains and trolleys

miniature golf, 111, 125, 178

Mt. Kendal, 125-126, 178

music, 127-129; Musical Union, The Oberlin, 126-127

Neighbor to neighbor committee, 53

New Russia Township, 33-34, 138

New York Times, The, 122

Newcomers Club, 67

Ninde Scholars Program, 72, 83

nursing care facilities, 32, 33, 35, 44,

Nutrition Committee, 51

Obamacare, *see* Affordable Care Act

Oberlin Clinic, 27

Oberlin College, 8, 15, 16, 18, 21, 80, 82, 83, 98, 125, 128, 129-130, 143, 153; "ExCo" courses, 130; Allen Memorial Art Museum, 130; Bonner Center for Service and Learning, 156; Illumination, 130; pottery Co-op, 104; Conservatory of Music, 76, 123, 127, 129

Oberlin Heritage Ctr., 76, 77, 82

Oberlin Inn, 1, 38

Oberlin News-Tribune, 133

Oberlin Public Library, 82

Oberlin Retirement Community, first meeting, 5-6; goals and criteria, 7; officers, 6, 13; incorporation, 11, 12; nonprofit status, 12; planning committee, vi, 2,

Ohio, state of, 15, 32-33

Oberlin Schools, 80-81, 83, 133, 143

Oberlin Senior Center, 86

Oberlin, city of, 14, 18, 33, 83, 129, 153

Oberlin, Kendal at, occupancy rates, 94

Ohio School Boards Association, 133

One to One Baking, *see* intergenerational activities

opening, challenges of, 41-45; ribbon-cutting, 42-43, 45

INDEX OF TOPICS   191

Organizing Council, *see* Residents Association

Penn, *see* dining areas
Phase I, II, III, *see* architecture
planning, 88-94
plant sale, 84
Play Readers, 131; Drama Circle, 131
Potluck, Staff-Resident, 140-141
pottery, *see* Ceramics
Publicity Plugs, 81, 133
putting green, *see* miniature golf

Quakers, *see* Friends, Religious Society of
quilts, 101

Radio broadcasts, 73
real estate planning, 10, 12, 15-17; planning, annexation, 33,; land acquisition, 33; land-use plan, 31; site selection, 17-18; utilities, 33
real estate prices, *see* economic trends
recession, *see* economic trends
recruitment, 24-26,
recycling, 50

residential units, (table), 97; assisted living, 32; independent living, 31
Residents Archives Committee, 157
Residents Assistance Fund, 11, 134; RAF Shop, 134-135, 179
Residents Association, Kendal at Oberlin (KORA), v, 50, 54-55, 102, 171; presidents, 171; structure, 54-55
residents, roster of, 163-170
retirement, ix; demographic trends, ix, 2-4, 29; economic trends, 3, 13-14, 85-88
Robert Burns Dinner, 136-137
Rock Pond, 65
Rockport, MA, *see* Lawn Chair Drill Team
Russia Township, *see* New Russia Township

Science Discussion Group, 137-138
Senior Independence, 90-91
shade garden, *see* Horticulture
Silliness Committee, 138-139
skilled nursing, *see* Stephens Care Center
social media, 94
Social Security, 155
Solstice, Winter, 149-150

SPINACH, 51, 139

Spring Fling, 139-140

SCC Shoppers, *see* Care and Concern Committee

staff recruitment, 37, 39

staff, long-serving, 172-174

Stephens Care Center, 48, 85, 90, 110, 117, 179-180; Jameson skilled nursing area, 177, 179; Patterson skilled nursing area, 179; Whittier assisted living units, 90, 152, 180

stretching/strengthening, *see* Exercise Group

student staff, *see* Dining Services

Supporting Friends, *see* Care and Concern Committee

Swarthmore College, 7

Sweetbriar College, 129

swimming pool, 32, 55-59

Table tennis, 142, 143-144

Tappan Square, 98, 135

tennis courts, 61

therapy garden, *see* Horticulture

Third Thursday Lecture Series, 145

time capsule, 66, 67

trains and trolleys, 145-148; Hoot 'n' Holler Railroad, 145-147; Milwaukee, WI, 147-148

Transportation Committee, 127

transportation, 147

Triangle Pond, 67

Trio, Kendal, 120-121

Troll Bridge, 148-149, 180

trustees, *see* directors

TV Committee, *Ad Hoc*, 68

Twilight Holiday Walk, 53-54,

Volunteering, 49

Weather, 41-42, 46,

weaving, 158

web site, residents', 118-120

wetlands, 19, 31,

Wheelchair Brigade, *see* Care and Concern Committee

whirligig, 68, 69, 104-105

Whittier assisted living, *see* Stephens Care Center

Wildflower Hill, *see* Mt. Kendal

William Penn Room, *see* dining areas

Woodland Pond, 65

Woodshop, 78, 106, 150-151

World Wide Web, 94, 118

INDEX OF TOPICS 193

Index of Names

Adams, Margaret Ellen, 160, 163

Ailey, Mary Frances ("Frampie"), 50, 160, 163

Ailey, Robert J., 160

Albright, Marilyn ("Lyn"), 163

Aldrich, Elizabeth, 122, 163

Allen, Sarah, 172

Anderson, David, 161

Anderson, Madeleine ("Molly"), 50, 161, 163

Anderson, Susan, 175

Andrews, George, 163, 175

Andrews, Marlene, 163

Appleton, Linda S., 161

Appleton, Lloyd O., 161

Arbogast, Bo, 156

Arnold, Paul B., 98, 100, 102, 161, 181

Arnold, Sarah C. ("Sally"), 98, 161

Arthur, Margaret R., 161

Ashbrook, Mary, 163, 171

Auble, Laura, 90, 172

Augustine, Mary, 163

Bacon, Agnes K., 163

Bacon, Cathryn, 120, 163

Bacon, Roger, 125

Baker, Ruth S., 160

Baldwin, Helen, 163

Baldwin, Robert ("Bob"), 163

Ballantyne, Duncan, 131

Balogh, Sara C., 79, 159

Barna, Barbara, 163

Barnett, Naomi, 163

Bassett, Virginia Ruth, 159

Baughman, Barbara, 163

Baum, Marian H., 160

Baznik, Donna, viii, 102, 163

Baznik, Richard, 163

Beauchamp, Nancy, 114, 163

Becher, Robyn, 174

Bent, George, 56, 109, 163, 175

Bent, Ruth Schoeni, 109, 163

Berner, Jeanne, 163

Berner, Jerome ("Jerry"), 110, 114, 131, 142, 163

Beveridge, Linda, 173

Bimber, Constance ("Connie"), 102, 163

Bimber, Russell, 163

Blackford, Lisa, 173

Blair, Kimberly, 173

Blodgett, Jane, 163

Blount, Viola, 131, 163

Boase, Constance ("Connie") W. Flanigan, 35, 56, 59, 159, 181, 183

Boase, Marjorie B., 159

Boase, Paul H., 159

Bockmore, Sandra, 173

Bolland, Janet, 84, 163

Bolland, Thomas W., 163

Bolyard, Rebecca, 172

Bojanowski, Carol, 175

Boren, Wynona, 163

Brantford, Majoretta, 173

Brashares, Charles M., 160

Brashares, Edith O., 160

Breese, Louise, 163

Brinkman, Elizabeth, 163

Brittingham, Midge, 175

Brown, Catharine ("Katie"), 41, 131, 163

Brown, Darlene, 173

Browne, Errol, 175

Bruer, Barbara, 163

Buck, Jane, 161

Buell, Jane, 121

Burgess, Liz, 175

Burkhard, Barbara Daschbach, 164

Burkhard, Richard, 164

Burton, Anne H., 109, 161

Busiel, Joanne, 164

Butler, Becky, vi, 172

Byles, G. Huntington, 160

Byles, Janet K., 160

Cady, Henry, 70

Canalos, G. Virginia, 160

Cardinal, Kimberly, 107

Carlson, Florence ("Bobbie"), 164

Carlson, Frank, 11, 12

Carlton, Claudine, 133, 164

Carlton, Terry, 102, 164

Carrell, Demaris ("Demmie"), vii, 7, 48, 72, 164, 181

Carrell, Jeptha ("Jep"), vii, xii, 5, 6, 7, 11, 12, 30, 72, 175

Carroll, Alan, 133, 152, 164

Carroll, Polly, 101, 152, 164

Carson, Marilyn, 164

Champney, Kathlyn B., 161

Chisholm, Corning, 164

Christie, Bettie L., 160

Clark, David, xii, 6, 10, 15, 16, 17, 18, 19, 24, 42, 164, 175, 181

Clark, Eleanor Stabler, ix

Clark, Jon, 175

Clark, Ricarda ("Ricky"), 164

Clark, Ruth Ann, 136, 164

Coan, Cynthia, 164

Coan, Robert, 164

Coffin, Frances D., 159

Coffin, Kenneth P., 159

Collins, Charlotte, 164

Comerford, Jennifer, 173

Connone, Jill, 172

Cook, Dennis, 164

Cook, Judy, 164

Cook, Margaret J., 161

Cooke, Vera, 164

Cooper, Frances ("Fran"), 84, 164

Cooper, Nancy, 164

Cooper, Roger, 164

Cotabish, Alice M., 160

Cothran, Robert, 150, 164

Culbert, Harvey, 118, 164

Cunningham, Anne, 37, 66

Current, Phyllis, 127, 160, 164

Custer, Benjamin A. ("Ben"), 42, 45, 122, 159

Custer, Emiko H., 45, 159, 164

Daffin, Norma, 49, 160, 164

David, Betsy, 164

David, Martin ("Tin"), 164

Davidoff, Martin, 164, 183

Davis, Anne, 164

DeBouter, Vance, 175

Deisinger, Loraine, 16,

Deist, Marcia, 164

Dembek, Joseph, 172

Dettman, Eileen, 70, 76, 140, 164

Devereux, Eleanor, 164

DeWitt, Betty, 164

DeWitt, William ("Bill"), 69, 104

Dexter, Lewis, 162

Didchenko, Rostislav ("Rosti"), 164

Diedrik, Laura, 173

Diffey, John, 42

Distelhorst, Garis, 175

Dixon, Elizabeth M., 161

Donner, Mae Alice, 164

Dugan, Joyce S., 161, 163

Dunn, Arlene, 164

Dunn, Larry, 164

Dunn, Richard J., 74, 175

Dupee, Laurie, 172

Durrett, Charles, 39

Dye, Nancy, 175

Eaton, Jean, 117, 164

Eckstein, Bernard, 165

Eckstein, Sheila, 165

Eddy, Ernest, 78, 135, 136, 151, 160, 165

Eddy, Jane, vii, viii, 102, 131, 160, 165, 171

Edgerton, John, 175

Edwards, Diann, 37

Elder, Anne Cartmel, 165

Elder, John, v, vii, viii, xii, 6, 11, 16, 35, 165, 171, 175, 181, 183

Ellenberger, Janette, 165

Ellis, Margaret-Ann, 108, 109, 136, 137, 165

Ellis, Milton, 108, 109, 165

Emerick, Jeffrey, 173

Erdy, Virgina, 164

Ernst, Joan K., 160

Evans, David, 70, 160, 165

Evans, Marie, 165

Evans, Mary C. ("Paulie"), 124, 160, 165

Farnsworth, Charles, 161

Farnsworth, Kathryn, 161, 165

Farquhar, Leslie, 139

Farquhar, William, 165

Fauver, Catherine, 165

Fell, Margaret, 177, 178

Ferguson, Janet, 165

Fischer, Gay, 165

Fisk, Mary W., 161
Flanigan Boase, Constance ("Connie") W., *see* Boase
Fletcher, Michael, 165
Flynt, Mary A., 160
Fordyce, Beverly, 165
Fordyce, Stuart, 165
Foreman, Marion B., 160
Foster, Janice, 173
Fox, George, 177, 178
France, Evelyn, 175
Freas, Pauline, 165
Freed, Nancy, 37, 133, 172
Freedman, James O., 14
Friedman, Edward, 1645
Friedman, Lois C., 165
Frierson, Andrew, 165
Fries, Terry, 37
Funkhouser, Mary L., 110, 159
Fuquay, Monica, 173

Gabalac, Frieda, 48, 161
Gage, Alan, 50, 52, 54, 148, 149, 151, 160, 165, 171, 180
Gage, Nancy, 102, 148, 149, 160, 165, 180

Gail, Debora, 174
Gallagher, Eugene, 165
Gallagher, Marilyn, 165
Ganzel, Carol, 165
Gardner, Daniel, 175
Garrett, Jane, 165
Garrett, Milton, 131, 165
Garver, Leonard , 78, 104, 135, 147, 148, 165
Garver, Nancy Bradford, 101, 124, 135, 165
Geissal, Marjorie N., 161
Giacobbe, Lynne, 174
Gladieux, Bernard L., 161
Gold, Margaret, 165
Goldberg, Marcia, 113, 165
Goldberg, Samuel, 136, 165
Gordon, John, 165
Gordon, Peggy, 165
Graf, Ruth, 131,
Graham, Jean Susan, 165
Greenberg, Eva, 133
Greenberg, Nathan ("Nate"), 165
Grove, Mary Lynne, 165

Haessly, Rita, 165
Hall, Crystal, 174
Hall, Jon, 172
Hallock, Jeffrey, 161
Hallock, Myriam L., 161
Hallock, Richard R., 161
Hamilton, Duane, 37
Hamilton, Jim, 50, 165
Handman, Pauline, 108, 165
Hannaford, R. Ogden, 55, 56
Hannauer, George, 165
Hannauer, Jane S., 76, 120, 165
Hanson, Ruth E., 103, 161
Haber, Mary, 175
Harley, Roy G. ("Dutch"), 114
Hasse, Frances S., 161
Hasse, Gordon W., 161
Hatton, Howard, 166
Hayes, Ardith, 124, 166
Hayward, Shirley, 52, 166, 181
Hayward, William ("Bill") 68, 73, 83, 148, 181
Heath, Elaine, 160
Heckert, Marcia, 23, 28, 36, 37
Hefner, Leslie ("Lee"), 166
Hefner, Robert, 166

Heiser, Karl, xii, 2, 4, 6, 7, 8, 11, 13, 18, 19, 35, 175, 177
Heiser, Ruth, xii, 4, 19, 177
Helke, Katherine, 173
Heller, Jean, 166
Helm, Annemarie ("Anne"), 166, 175
Helm, James, 113, 151 166
Helper, Eleanor, 166
Henke, Herbert, 166
Henke, Sabra C., 166
Herrick, Kay, 2003
Hewitt, David, 24, 175
Hill-Holcomb, Patricia, 173
Histed, Margaret E., 160
Hodgson, Cornelia C., 31, 59
Hoerr, Janet U., 160
Hoffman, Michael, 175
Hoffman, Therese, 37
Hoffmann, Randi, 166
Hofman, Feite ("Fred"), 166
Holbrook, Dorothy ("Dot") B., 46, 54, 67, 159
Holliman, James, 176
Holzhauer, Dorothy, 172
Howard, Saun, 140

Hull, Shirley, 16

Hultquist, Donald, 112, 114, 139, 166, 181

Hultquist, Nancy S., 106, 112, 114, 139, 140, 166, 171, 181

Hunt, Alan, 7, 8, 9, 11, 13

Hunt, Esther C., 44, 45, 46, 67, 159, 166

Huszti, Allen, 127, 129, 148, 166

Hutchison, Janet B., 159, 166, 176

Hutchison, William M., 159

Ijiri, Tomoko, 166

Ijiri, Yuji, 166

Illig, Donald, 82, 166

Illig, Joylynn ("Joy"), 166

Ingersoll, Fern, 108, 166

Ingersoll, Jay, 108, 166

James, Elizabeth ("Betty"), 92, 166

Jameson, George, C., 177

Jasko, Ruth, 173

Jenkins, Adelbert ("Del"), 92, 118, 166

Jenkins, Betty, 166

Jensen, Ann, xii, 176

Johnson, Mayo Crew, 57

Johnson, Patricia, 173

Johnson, Jr., William ("Bill") C., 57, 161

Jones, Eddythe M., 159

Jones, Owen T., 160

Jones, Robin, 174

Kahn, Diana, 166

Kahn, Ron, 166

Kane, Ellen, 161

Kanost, Margaret, 166

Kay, Marvin ("Mike"), 166

Keating, Susan, 176

Keeney, Elizabeth, 176

Kellner, Eileen, 166

Ketcham, Helen, 166

Kinley, John, 176

Knight, Roderic ("Rod"), 125, 147, 148

Koeblitz, William ("Bill"), xii, 13, 176

Koerner, Gerlind, 81, 166

Kohl, Alice, 166

Kornblith, Ina Jean, 48

Koster, Mary, 166
Kovach, Terry, vi, 173
Krato, Darlene, 166
Krislov, Marvin, 176
Kroupa, Debbie, 37
Kuncel, Susan, 173
Kurtz. Edith M., 160

Laird, Bert, 114
Laird, Hallie, 113, 114, 177
Laird, Helen E., 160
Laird, John H., 160
Lamb, Harold, 166
Lancaster, Sydney, 176
Langeler, George, 166
Langston, John Mercer, 178
Lanham, Theresa (Terri), 172
Lapham, Lowell, 162
Largent, Robert M., 159
Largent, Vera M., 159
Laurell, Gaye, 166
LeBeau, Constance J., 160
LeBeau, Marjorie M., 160
LeGrand, Raymond, 166
Lenz, Benjamin, 106, 107, 108, 125, 131, 139, 167
Lenz, Pamela, 108, 114, 125, 131, 139, 167
Leonard, Barbara, 50, 107, 161
Leonard, Margaret, 161
Lester, Catharina ("Katy") D., 160, 167
Lewis, Arn, 102, 167
Lewis, Beth, 102, 167
Lewis, Erin, 176
Lewis, Irwin ("Irv"), 167
Lewis, Lloyd, xii, 7, 8, 10, 13, 15, 23, 24, 26, 30, 31, 34, 35, 36, 55
Lewis, Mary Jane, 160
Licklider, Adelaide, 161
Licklider, Templin, 161
Lilie, Ellen Anna, 161
Lindamood, Jane, 167
Lindner, Deborah, 174
Livingston, Dayton, 176
Long, Bill, xii, 5, 167
Long, Charlotte R., 159, 167
Long, Edward, 167
Long, Herbert S., 159, 167
Long, James, 176

Long, Russell ("Rusty"), 167
Longsworth, Carol, 167
Longsworth, Robert, 167
Lott, Marian J., 127, 167
Loudermelt, Blair, 173
Love, Duncan, 102, 151
Love, Nina, 80, 167
Luciano, Dorothy, xii, 5, 7, 14, 15, 35, 55, 65, 72, 154, 167, 176, 182
Luciano, Joseph, 125, 154, 167, 171, 176
Lucioli, Clara E., 110, 161
Luckenbill, Louise, 167

MacKay, Gladys G., 42, 161
MacKay, James A., 42, 161
Marshall, Elizabeth ("Betty"), 167
Marshall, Jim, 167
Marshall, Linda, 167
Martin, Anne, 167
Martin, Tom, 167
Martinez, Elizabeth, 173
Martz, Pradnya, 176
Mason, Emma, 176

Maurushat, Jocelyn, 167
McCalla, Mary Beth, 167
McCamant, Kathryn, 39
McClusky, Nancy, 167
McClusky, Robert, 167
McCord, Diana, 14, 16, 20, 26, 36
McCorkle, Hugh F., 53, 118, 160
McCorkle, Lois P., 53, 160, 167
McCullough, David, v
McCullough, Dennis, 96
McIlroy, Amy, 162
McIlroy, Donald, 162
McKee, Mary, 176
McQueen, Albert, 167
Meese, William, 176
Meints, Nelle G., 48, 161
Melcher, Anna S., 161
Melecki, Richard, 176
Merleno, Toni, vi, 173
Merritt, Helen K., 159
Metcalf, Sarah H., 161
Metzger, G. Herbert, 161
Metzger, Madelyn L., 161
Meyer, Kevin, 107

Michalak, Bernice, 167

Mihu, Jean, 167

Miller, Ed, 176

Miller, Judith, 172

Miller, Ruth, 167

Miller, Tom, 41

Milliken, Elizabeth, 160

Milliken, Elizabeth D., 160

Miraldi, Mary K., 143, 160

Mitchell, Tom, 34

Mitro, Eleanor, 162

Moore, Jane H., 42, 159

Moore, Jane Ross, 167

Moore, Samuel ("Sam") A., 42, 151, 159

Moreland, Jean, 167

Morgan, Maxwell G., 109, 159, 167

Morgan, Muriel P., 109, 159, 167

Morris, Thelma J., 107, 133, 167, 183

Mosher, Harriet J., 161

Murphy, Jerry, 167

Myerly, Joyce, 167

Myerly, Richard, 167

Myerson, Marilyn, 84, 167

Neavill, Elizabeth B., 161

Neill, Elizabeth M., 161

Nickles, Jean, 173

Ninde, Nancy ("Nan"), 72, 83

Ninde, Richard ("Dick"), 72, 83

Nizza, Jane, 176

Nord, Jane, 120, 167

Norenberg, Don, 167

Norenberg, Joanne, 111, 168

Norton, Jane, 176

Nowick, Theodore, 140, 168

Nunley, Katherine, 116, 168

O'Connor, Elizabeth, 167

O'Malley, Ann, 174

O'Neil, June, 168

O'Toole, Dennis, 176

Olmsted, Clarence ("Bush"), 168

Olmsted, Levona, 168

Oncley, Paul, 126, 127

Orcutt, Adrienne ("Adie"), 168

Orcutt, Scott, 168

Palmer, JoDee, vi, 173

Palmieri, Joseph, 168

Palmieri, Susan, 168

Paré, Diantha, 168

Paré, Victor, 168

Parker, Don, 108, 114, 115, 145, 146, 147, 168

Parker, Joyce, 104, 108, 115, 145, 168

Parrott, Anne, 168

Patterson, David, 173

Patterson, Mary Jane, 179

Payton, Eileen, 168

Payton, John, 168

Pech, Keith, 143

Peck, M. Scott, 23

Penn, William, 179

Perhamus, Ernest, 168

Pesuit, Harol, 168

Pesuit, John, 148, 168

Peterson, Carl, 119, 168

Peterson, Lois G., 50, 160

Piccinini, Anne, 37

Picken, John, 175, 176

Pilisy, Ann, 39, 141, 143, 172, 182

Piraino, Tom, x, 18, 54, 157, 171, 175, 176, 182

Podwalny, Sandra, 52

Poporad, Anna, 161

Porter, Larry, 168

Porter, Marjorie, 168

Potter, Ann, 102, 168

Prescott, Katherine, 110, 161

Prescott, Polly, 161

Preston, Kim, 173

Price, Julie, 172

Protzman, Ferdinand, 176

Protzman, Tom, 137

Pugsley, Emily, 168

Pugsley, James, 119, 168

Putnam, Robert, 23

Ramp, Marjorie, 176

Randel, Helen, 168

Randel, Robert, 168

Reed, Melissa, 168

Reed, Tim, 41

Reeves, Barbara, 168

Reeves, Don, viii, 156, 168, 171

Regli, Constance W., 159

Reiber, Daniel, 108, 148, 168

Reichard, Anita, vi, vii, xii, 1, 5, 6, 7, 8, 9, 10, 11, 12, 13, 14, 22, 24, 25, 42, 161, 176

Reichard, Joseph, 8, 22, 24, 161
Reid, Margaret ("Peggy"), 113, 168
Renfrow, Antoinette S., 160
Renfrow, William ("Bill") B., 61, 144, 160
Reynolds, Harriet, 159
Rice, Mary Jean, 168
Rice, William, 168, 176
Richards, Louise S., 102, 160, 168
Ricker, Alison, 176
Rider, Margaret ("Kay"), 168
Rimbert, Jennifer, 173
Ricker, Alison, 176
Rivers, Therese, 176
Rogers, Suzanne, 173
Rollin, Kimberly, 173
Rollins, Susanne, 174
Roose, Diana, 6, 176
Roose, Gretchen, 113, 161, 168
Roose, Kenneth, 61, 144, 161, 168
Rosen, Michael, 123
Rosenfeld, Sidney, 143, 168
Rosenfeld, Stella, 168
Rotermund, F. Elisabeth, 161
Runyan, Elizabeth, 70, 162
Runyan, William, 162
Rutherford, Isobel, 168

Sabath, Nancy, 175, 176
Sable, Doris S., 62, 110, 161
Saxon, Phyllis, 173
Schaal, David, 168
Schaal, Jean S., 168
Schaeffer, Eunice B., 160, 168
Schaeffer, K. H., 160
Schaeffer, Ruth, 171
Schneider, Alverta, 168
Schoonmaker, Dina, 169, 183
Schoonmaker, Richard, 168
Schreiner, Kathryn, 169
Schreiner, William, 95, 105, 106, 169
Schultz, Margaret ("Peg"), 101, 169
Schultz, Trina, 37
Schumate, Regina, 173
Schuster, Melvin, 169
Schwaegerle, Catherine ("Cate"), 169
Schwaegerle, Edward G., vii, xii, 13, 14, 20, 160, 169, 176

Schwaegerle, Paul, 125, 169
Schwaegerle, Ruth C., 20, 90, 135, 160, 169
Schwartz, Howard, 169
Schwimmer, Helen M., 159, 184
Searles, Ruth, 133, 169
Shaeffer, Ruth, 63, 176
Shaver, Alice, 149, 162
Shaw, Julia, 169
Shearer, John, 169
Shearer, Mary Ann, 169
Shields-Kyle, Eldonna, 176
Shoemaker, Louise, 169
Simons, Mary, 169
Simonson, Roy W., 160
Simonson, Susan M., 160
Simpson, Alice H., 161
Simpson, Eleanor, 1, 2
Simpson, George, 1, 2
Singleton, Robert, 176
Singer, Leonard, 104, 169, 171
Singleton, Robert C., 160
Singleton, Wanda R., 160
Slajnar, Millie, 160
Smith, Audra C., 160
Smith, Donna, 148
Smith, Miriam Waldron, 161
Smith, William ("Bob"), 109
Sook, Lois, 102, 169
Spelman, Elizabeth L., 118, 160
Spelman, Gordon, 160
Spelman, Kathleen M., 160
Spierling, Paul ("Bud"), 108, 114, 169
Sprigg, Patricia, xii, 24, 26, 35, 36, 37
Springfield, Freddie, 176
Sprow, Clementine H., 159
Stacy, Martha, 133, 169
Stalzkowski, Ryan, 174
Stark, Maggie, vi, 66, 172, 182
Starr, S. Frederick, 17, 21, 24, 42
Stechow, Ursula, 161
Steele, Arthur ("Art") R., 50, 121, 149, 161
Steele, Elizabeth ("Libby"), 131, 161
Steinberg, Ira, 86, 169
Steinberg, Priscilla, vii, 145, 148, 169, 183
Stephens, James ("Jim") T., xii, 6, 7, 11, 12, 13, 14, 17, 18, 24, 63, 159, 175, 176, 179

Stephens, Jeanne H., 27, 52, 159, 179

Stevenson, Nicholas, 149, 160

Stewart, Lisa, 174

Stiles, Elizabeth W., 161

Stilwell, David, 176

Stocker, Beth K., 160

Stonestreet, Scott, 136, 137

Stunkel, Eva, 169

Sunshine, James, 169

Sutton, Stephanie, 174

Svete, Irene E., 159

Swank, Coby, 131

Swartwout, June, 102, 169

Talbot, Patricia, 148, 169

Tandy, Judith, 169

Tarsitano-Amato, Michele, 41, 43, 103, 110, 156, 172, 182

Taylor, Helen, 150, 169

Taylor, Richard W., 55, 160

Taylor, Robert, viii. 99, 106, 107, 110, 169, 171, 176

Taylor, Sadie W., 48, 50, 55, 160, 176

Terrell, Stacy, 96

Thomas, Barbara, vi, 24, 34, 36, 37, 39, 42, 47, 48, 50, 56, 57, 133, 172, 182

Thomas, Robert, 2, 6, 176

Thomas, Elizabeth ("Betsy"), 122, 169, 176

Thompson, Catherine, 169

Thompson, Priscilla E., 161

Thomson, Mary Lou, 40

Tibbetts, Katherine K., 159

Tibbetts, William D., 159

Tolbert, Melva, 175, 176

Tompos, Grace, 169

Treuhaft, Paul, 176

Trump, Richard, 169

Turner, Ralph, 118, 137, 162, 169, 182

Valentine-Byrd, Bonnie, 174

VanDale, Carla, 169

VanDale, Robert, 169

VanDyke, Don P., vi, 37, 104, 110, 122, 162, 169, 182, 183

VanDyke, Mary Louise, 104, 158, 162, 169

VanRaaphorst, Donna, 169

Verlie, E. Joseph (Joe), 50, 54, 159, 171

Verlie, Elizabeth E. (Betty), 49, 104, 159

Wagner, Helen, 161

Waite, Jan, 176

Walker, Barry, 169

Walker, Mary Emma, 107, 162

Walker, William, 162

Walworth, Frank, 169

Walworth, Joy, 169

Wanyek, Janet, 170

Warch, Pauline ("Polly") R., 50, 161

Warch, Willard F., 161

Wardwell, Anne, 92, 108, 170

Wardwell, Edward, 92, 108, 170

Watson, Renee, 85

Webb, William H., 90

Weber, Wilma, 120, 170

Webster, Jane, 174

Webster, Tori, 174

Weigl, Etta Ruth, 50, 56, 57, 59, 133, 160, 170

Weinberg, Herbert, 170

Weinstock, Elizabeth B. ("Betty"), 6, 85, 126, 131, 144, 160, 170

Weinstock, Robert ("Bob"), 122, 160

Werner, Janet Kelsey, 170

Werner, R. Budd, 170

Wheeler, Margaret, 170

White, Bonnie, 172

White, Calvin, 24

White, James ("Jim") W., 133, 160

Whitehead, Eleanor, 170

Whittier, John Greenleaf, 180

Wickes, Warren, 170

Wilber, Catherine, 170

Wilcox, Anne, 170

Wilcox, Dorothy H., 161

Wilcox, George, 170

Wiles, Stephanie, 176

Wilgor, Gregory, 174

Wolf, Virginia, 173

Worcester, Florence E., 160

Wright, Elizabeth L., 159

Wright, Glen, 136, 137

Wright, Jean F., 16, 161, 170

Yerkes, Kathe, 182

Ybarra, Ramie, 172

Yinger, Milton ("Milt"), 50, 162

Yinger, Winnie, 50, 162

Yood, Nancy 176

Young, Evelyn, 134, 159

Young, Keith R., 159, 176

Young, Victoria ("Torie") K., 48, 111, 159, 170

Zeitlin, Aideen, 170

Zeitlin, Gerald, 170

Zimmerman, Beverly, 172

Zinn, Grover, 170

Zinn, Mary, 170

Zitani, May, 114, 139, 170

About the Book

The main text for this book is typeset in 12 point Source Sans Pro, a font designed in recent years by Paul D. Hunt in collaboration with Adobe Systems, Inc. It was selected because studies conducted by the American Publishing House, a leading contributor to improving access to text for low-vision readers, strongly recommends a sans serif face rather than a serif face, the more traditional choice for a book project. Source Sans Pro's letterforms offer readability along with a measure of elegance, thus meeting the design criteria for this project on several fronts.

Major headings are set in Palatino, a font initially designed by Herman Zapf in 1948 for the Linotype Foundry and refined by him with other collaborators in later years. Selected portions of these headings are set in a variant adapted specifically for Kendal.

The book was designed by the author using Adobe InDesign CS6 and related software, installed on an Apple Mac Pro.

Photographs came from several sources, most notably Kendal's administrative offices, other residents, and from the stored images used to celebrate previous anniversaries. Where the photographer can be identified, he or she is credited in the caption. In addition, the author contributed many photographs.

The book was produced at Bookmasters, Inc., located in Ashland, Ohio, using a digital printing process.